بسم الله الرحمن الرحيم

الله

إِهْدَاءُ ثَوَابِ القُرآنِ وَالطَّاعَاتِ إِلَى الأَمْوَاتِ

DEDICATING REWARDS TO THE DECEASED

Reciting the Qur'ān & Other Good Deeds

Shaykh Muḥammad Fawāz an-Nimr
Imam and Teacher at the Umayyad Grand Masjid in Damascus

With Appendices from
Imam Jalāl ad-Dīn as-Suyūṭī
Imam Yaḥyā an-Nawawī
Imam Wahbah az-Zuḥaylī رحمهم الله

Translated by
Mahdi Lock

NAWA BOOKS
THE FOREWORD PUBLICATIONS

We at The Foreword Publications and Nawa Books would like to express our appreciation to everybody who contributed in making this book a reality. We pray that Allah ﷻ bestow His blessings upon it by guiding readers of this book closer towards Allah ﷻ and His beloved Prophet Muhammad ﷺ.

Dedicating Rewards to the Deceased: Reciting the Qurʾān & Other Good-Deeds by Shaykh Muḥammad Fawāz an-Nimr, Imam and Teacher at the Umayyad Grand Masjid in Damascus
إِهْدَاءُ ثَوَابِ القُرآنِ وَالطَّاعَاتِ إِلَى الْأَمْوَاتِ

Published by:	Nawa Books & The Foreword Publications
Published in:	May 2023
Author:	Shaykh Muḥammad Fawāz an-Nimr
Translated by:	Mahdi Lock

ISBN:	978-981-18-7035-4
Cover by:	Muhammadan Press

Contents

Translator's Introduction & Acknowledgements

All praise belongs to Allah, Lord of all creation, who forgives sins and with Him alone is every success. There is no power or strength except in Him. As Allah has honoured this miserable slave with the completion of such a task, all I ask is that He increase the blessings He has already bestowed upon me and to make me a better believer, cleanse my heart and grant me further strength to serve Him and the Ummah of His Beloved, *ṣallā Allahu ʿalayhi wa sallam.*

As for the creation, I begin by thanking Shaykh Muḥammad Fawāz for granting permission to translate and publish this book. The shaykh is an extremely dedicated teacher, as can be seen by anyone who visits his YouTube channel, so it was truly a blessing to speak to him briefly online and ask him for permission. He then sent me his curriculum vitae when I was unable to find a biography of him. May Allah reward him immensely in this life and the next, amīn!

I also ask Allah to bless and reward Dr Maḥmūd Ramaḍān for speaking to the author and giving me his phone number, and for administering the ever-so-useful Naseem al-Sham site, from where I downloaded a copy of the book.

Then there is Ustādh Muhammad Jalaluddeen of Nawa Books, who agreed to publish the book in partnership with The Foreword Publications and take care of the typesetting and cover design. If Allah so wills, this is only the first of many such projects. May Allah reward him in abundance, amīn!

Then there is proofreading. I ask Allah to bless and reward my dear friend Iskander Gani for examining the text meticulously and pointing out several typographical errors. Furthermore, I ask Allah to shower his beloved grandmother with mercy and forgiveness and to grant her a lofty rank in Paradise; her Lord called her home between his proofreading and the publication of the book. Allah works in wonderful ways. Brother Iskander was able to benefit from the contents before anyone else, which means his grandmother should also be benefitting. Glory be to Allah!

I would also like to thank the contemporary master of English grammar, Neville Gwynne, for helping me render one particularly difficult sentence. We had to exchange quite a few emails before settling on a final rendition.

Lastly, I thank my wife for her patience, serenity, and encouragement throughout the translation process. May Allah reward her and her parents immensely, āmīn!

The book in your hands is an attempt to put an end to a debate that actually ended several centuries ago. That is, it ended among the ʿulamāʾ, those who are qualified to speak on the matter, and yet, for some reason, it has been revived in recent times. As you will see in the book and in the appendices, the early generations did indeed differ over whether the reward for reciting the Qurʾān reached the deceased, but over time they came to be of one accord: the reward for reciting the Qurʾān does indeed reach the deceased and it is the *muʿtamad* position of all Four Schools.

These words of Imam as-Suyūṭī in *Sharḥ as-Ṣudūr*, which are quoted in Appendix A, make this very clear:

> [The ʿulamāʾ] also infer from the aḥādīth that mention it, even though they are weak, for their sum total indicates that there is a foundation. Furthermore, the Muslims in every big city still gather together and recite for the benefit of their deceased

without any reproach. Thus, it is a consensus. All of this has been mentioned by al-Ḥāfiẓ Shams ad-Dīn ibn ʿAbdul Wāḥid al-Maqdasī al-Ḥanbalī in a volume he wrote on the issue.

Al-Qurṭubī said, 'Ash-Shaykh ʿIzz ad-Dīn ibn ʿAbdis Salām would issue *fatāwā* stating the reward for what one recites does not reach the deceased. When he had died, one of his companions saw him, so he said to him, "You used to say the reward for what one recites does not reach the deceased and is not gifted to him, so how is it?" He replied, "I used to say that in the abode of the world. Now, I have gone back on my position after seeing Allah's magnanimity therein and that it does reach him".'

And with Allah alone is every success.

May Allah have mercy on all believers, the living and the deceased, and may He make the former a source of constant benefit and relief for the latter, amīn!

Mahdi Lock
1 Ramadan 1444

About the Author

Shaykh Muḥammad Fawāz an-Nimr, may Allah preserve him, is one of the leading Ḥanafī teachers of this age, based in Damascus. He graduated from Maʿhad al-Fatḥ al-Islāmī in 1985 and in the following year took up teaching posts at that institute as well as at the Umayyad Grand Masjid. Since then, he has taught several books, including:

- *Qaṭr an-Nadā*
- *Sharḥ Ibn ʿAqīl*
- *Awḍaḥ al-Masālik li Sharḥ Alfiyyat Ibn Mālik*
- *Jāmiʿ ad-Durūs al-ʿArabiyyah*
- *Mughnī al-Labīb*
- *Iḥyāʾ ʿUlūm ad-Dīn*
- *Mawsūʿah at-Tafsīr al-Munīr fī al-ʿAqīdah wa ash-Sharīʿah wa al-Minhāj*
- *Tafsīr al-Qurṭubī (al-Jāmiʿ li Aḥkām al-Qurʾān)*
- *Al-Ikhtiyār li Taʿlīl al-Mukhtār*
- *Nuzhat al-Muttaqīn Sharḥ Riyāḍ as-Ṣāliḥīn*
- *Marāqī al-Falāḥ*
- *Ḥāshiyat at-Ṭaḥāwī*
- *Tāj al-Jāmiʿ lil-Uṣūl*
- *Nawādir al-Uṣūl*
- *Tanbīh al-Mughtarīn*
- *Ash-Shifā bi Taʿrīf Ḥuqūq al-Muṣṭafā* ﷺ
- *Sayyiduna Muḥammad Rasūl Allāh* ﷺ
- *As-Ṣalāt ʿAla an-Nabī* ﷺ
- *At-Tajrīd as-Ṣarīḥ*
- *Al-Īmān bi ʿAwālim al-Ākhirah*

- *Tāj al-ʿUrūs*
- *Al-Lubāb Sharḥ al-Kitāb*
- *Ṣiffat as-Ṣafwah*
- *Ṣafwat at-Tafāsīr*
- *Mukhtaṣar Minhāj al-Qāṣidīn*
- *At-Targhīb wa at-Tarhīb*
- *Nūr al-Īḍāḥ*
- *Tafsīr an-Nasafī*

His Teachers Include the Following:

- Shaykh Ṣālih al-Farfūr, the founder of Maʿhad al-Fatḥ
- Shaykh ʿAbdur Razzāq al-Ḥalabī
- Shaykh Adīb Kallās
- Shaykh Aḥmad Quttābi
- Shaykh Suhayl az-Zabībī
- Shaykh Aḥmad Ramaḍān
- Shaykh Muwaffaq an-Nashūqātī
- Shaykh Ḥussām ad-Dīn al-Farfūr
- Shaykh Walī ad-Dīn Farfūr
- Shaykh Ramzī al-Bazm and his son, Shaykh ʿAbdul Fattāḥ al-Bazm
- Shaykh ʿAbdul Mājid al-Ḥanāwī
- Shaykh Rajab Dīb
- Shaykh Muḥammad Saʿīd Ramaḍān al-Būṭī
- Shaykh Nūr ad-Dīn ʿItr
- Shaykh Luṭfī al-Fayūmī
- Shaykh Ṣāliḥ al-Ḥamawī
- Shaykh ʿAbdur Raḥmān ash-Shāghūrī
- Shaykh Bashīr Kirmān
- Shaykh Usāmah al-Khānī
- As-Sayyid Ibrāhīm al-Khalīfah al-Iḥsāʾī

Praise be to Allah, the shaykh's lessons are available on YouTube and several are uploaded daily to his channel: @MFawazAlnemer. May Allah grant the shaykh a long life filled with righteousness and good health, amīn!

About the Translator

Mahdi Lock is a professional freelance translator of classical Arabic Islamic texts into English. He has a BA in Arabic and History from the University of Leeds, an MA in Arabic Linguistics from King Abdul Aziz University in Jeddah, and a Diploma in Translation from the Chartered Institute of Linguists in London, of which he is also a Member (MCIL). He has been studying theology, law and other Islamic sciences for several years with teachers in England, North Africa and the Middle East.

To date, his translated works include:

- *Kitāb al-Ḥalāl wa al-Ḥarām* by Imam Abū Ḥāmid al-Ghazālī
- *Kitāb al-Waqf* from *al-Mughnī al-Muḥtāj* by al-Khaṭīb al-Shirbīnī
- The introduction to *al-Majmūʿ* by Imam Yaḥyā al-Nawawī
- *Sharḥ al-Ṣudūr* by Imam Jalāl al-Dīn al-Suyūṭī
- Almost 2000 pages of the *Khawāṭir* of Imam Muḥammad Mutawalli ash-Shaʿrawī (http://www.elsharawyreflections.com/)
- *La Dhukūriyyah fī al-Fiqh* by Imam Muḥammad at-Tāwīl
- *Manhaj al-Ḥaḍārah al-Insāniyyah fī al-Qurʾān* by Imam Muḥammad Saʿīd Ramaḍān al-Būṭī

For Nawa Books, he has translated the following:

- *Al-Wāfī: A Thorough Commentary on the Forty Nawawiyyah* by Imams Muṣṭafā al-Bughā and Muḥyī ad-Dīn Mistū
- *Man and Allah's Justice on Earth, Inward Sin, A Unique Pedagogical Approach in the Qur'ān, To Every Young Woman Who Believes in Allah, Islam and the Problems of the Youth*, all of which are part of the Pinnacle Papers series by Imam Muḥammad Saʿīd Ramaḍān al-Būṭī
- The first volume of *al-Fiqh al-Manhajī ʿalā Madhhab al-Imām ash-Shāfiʿī*, by Imams Muṣṭafā al-Bughā, Alī ash-Sharbajī, and Muṣṭafā al-Khin ﷺ
- *The Rights of the Husband and Wife* by Shaykh ʿAbdul Hādī al-Kharsah
- *Remembrances & Etiquettes of The Prophet* ﷺ

Mahdi has also been teaching English and Arabic for about two decades, from primary school through to the university level. He teaches other sciences privately, mainly fiqh, and regularly does online study circles, such as the Halaqah Book Club.

You can follow Mahdi online via his eponymous blog, where he posts translations of fatwas, khutbahs, articles, and other beneficial material, and his YouTube channel (@TheForeword), where he posts podcasts on various topics and translations from the classes and lectures of ʿulamā'.

بسم الله الرحمن الرحيم

In the Name of Allah, the All-Merciful, the Most Merciful

Praise be to Allah, the Most High, He who created and moulded, He who determined and guided,[1] who causes death and brings to life, who has made this world a seedbed for the Hereafter. And may the purest blessings and peace be upon the bearer of the most handsome guise and of the highest ranks, our master, Muḥammad the son of ʿAbdullah, and upon his Family, his Companions, and those who follow him.

To proceed:

Praise be to Allah for the blessing of Islam, and it suffices as a blessing. Praise be to Allah for making us from the Ummah of this Beloved ﷺ. Praise be to Allah for placing us upon the Right Way, the way of the Saved Sect,[2] and combined for us between love of his pure Family and love of his righteous Companions.

Praise be to Allah for this blessed assembly, which includes a number of luminaries from Muslim Orthodoxy[3] in order to elucidate the distinguishing characteristics of the Saved Sect, and to remove the sins of doubt from certain issues, doubts that are stirred up regarding certain fundamental and branch issues, and cause confusion for some people in the Ummah.

One of the issues that has had a lot of dust stirred up around it is the issue of deeds benefitting the deceased.

1 See Sūrat al-ʿAlā, 87:2-3.
2 Ar. *al-firqah an-nājiyah.*
3 Ar. *Ahl as-Sunnah wa al-Jamāʿah.*

If a person were to supplicate, recite the Noble Qurʾān, give to charity, or do any other act of worship and righteousness, and then dedicate the reward for that deed to someone deceased from this Ummah and ask Allah the Exalted to make it reach that deceased person, is such an action legitimate? And does the reward for that deed reach that deceased person?

The position of the majority of the Imams and the verifying scholars of Muslim Orthodoxy is that this action is legitimate and allowed, that gifting deeds to both the living and the dead is permissible, and that a person often benefits from the deeds of others.

By Allah the Exalted's Grace, I have divided this research paper into the following sections:

1. The legitimacy of this matter according to the totality of Muslim Orthodoxy, and the consensus of the Four Schools upon its legitimacy.

2. Mentioning some of the evidences for the legitimacy of this matter.

3. Citing some texts that clearly demonstrate the legitimacy of this matter from imams who are relied upon by those who hold a different view and attribute themselves to them.

The Legitimacy of This Matter According to the Totality of Muslim Orthodoxy & the Consensus of the Four Schools upon Its Legitimacy

Anyone who has looked into this matter objectively and impartially has discovered that this issue, in general, is one of agreement amongst Muslim Orthodoxy; no reliable scholar has ever differed with the foundation of its legitimacy. The difference of opinion is confined to the types of deeds. I shall prove this by presenting the relative texts from the books of fiqh and its sources according to Muslim Orthodoxy, which is represented by Ḥanafī Fiqh, Mālikī Fiqh, Shāfiʿī Fiqh, and Ḥanbalī Fiqh as established from Imam Aḥmad, may Allah the Exalted have mercy on him and be pleased with him.

I present to you, my noble brethren, some of these texts from the relied-upon[4] books of the Four Schools, and I shall cite them in chronological order, which means that I shall start with the Ḥanafī School, then the Mālikī School, then the Shāfiʿīs, and then the Ḥanbalīs.

4 Ar. *muʿtamad*.

The Ḥanafī School

Imam al-Marghīnānī says in *al-Hidāyah* in the chapter on performing the Ḥajj on behalf of others:

'The foundation in this chapter is that a person may dedicate the reward for his deed to someone else from Muslim Orthodoxy, whether that deed be a prayer, a fast, charity. This is due to what has been related from the Prophet ﷺ in which he sacrificed two black and white[5] rams, one for himself and the other on behalf of those of his Ummah who affirm Allah the Exalted's Oneness and testify that he has conveyed the Message. He sacrificed one of the two sheep for his Ummah.'[6]

Al-ʿAllāmah Ibn Nujaym says in *al-Baḥr ar-Rāʾiq Sharḥ Kanz ad-Daqāʾiq*:

'(The chapter on performing the Ḥajj on behalf of others) The foundation is that a person may dedicate the reward for his deed to someone else, whether that deed be a prayer, a fast, charity, recitation of the Qurʾān, *dhikr*, a circumambulation[7] of the Kaʿbah, a Ḥajj, an ʿUmrah, or anything else according to our companions. This is due to what is found in both the Book and the Sunnah. As for the Book, it is the Exalted One's words:

---

5 Ar. *amlaḥ*, which may mean speckled or spotted.

6 *Al-Hidāyah fī Sharḥ Bidāyat al-Mubtadī*, 1:178, the chapter on performing the Ḥajj on behalf of others.

7 Ar. *ṭawāf*.

﴿وَقُل رَّبِّ ٱرْحَمْهُمَا كَمَا رَبَّيَانِي صَغِيرًا﴾

"Lord, show mercy to them as they did in looking after me when I was small." [al-Isrā' 17:24]

'The Exalted One also tells us about the angels:

﴿وَيَسْتَغْفِرُونَ لِلَّذِينَ ءَامَنُوا...﴾

"...and ask forgiveness for those who believe." [Ghāfir 40:7]

'The Exalted One then quotes them by saying:

﴿رَبَّنَا وَسِعْتَ كُلَّ شَيْءٍ رَّحْمَةً وَعِلْمًا فَٱغْفِرْ لِلَّذِينَ تَابُوا وَٱتَّبَعُوا سَبِيلَكَ وَقِهِمْ عَذَابَ ٱلْجَحِيمِ ۝٧ رَبَّنَا وَأَدْخِلْهُمْ جَنَّٰتِ عَدْنٍ ٱلَّتِي وَعَدتَّهُمْ وَمَن صَلَحَ مِنْ ءَابَآئِهِمْ وَأَزْوَٰجِهِمْ وَذُرِّيَّٰتِهِمْ ۚ إِنَّكَ أَنتَ ٱلْعَزِيزُ ٱلْحَكِيمُ ۝٨ وَقِهِمُ ٱلسَّيِّـَٔاتِ...﴾

"Our Lord, you encompass everything in mercy and knowledge! Forgive those who turn to You and follow your Way and safeguard them from the punishment of the Blazing Fire. Our Lord, admit them to the garden of Eden You have promised them, and all of their parents, wifes and children who acted rightly. Truly You are the Almighty, the All-Wise. And safeguard them from evil acts...." [Ghāfir 40:7-9]

'As for the Sunnah, there are many ḥadīths. For example, in the two *Ṣaḥīḥ* collections, there is the ḥadīth in which he sacrificed two rams and dedicated one of them to his Ummah, and it is a well-known narration that provides more details for what is in the Book. There is also what has been related by Abū Dāwūd: {Recite Sūrat Yā Sīn over your deceased.} This means that the Exalted One's words:

﴿وَأَن لَّيْسَ لِلْإِنسَـٰنِ إِلَّا مَا سَعَىٰ﴾

"that man will have nothing but what he strives for" [an-Najm 53:39] cannot be understood according to its apparent purport.

'There are different interpretations, and the most correct of them is what was chosen by the verifying scholar Ibn al-Humām, which is that it is restricted to what the person doing the deed gifts. In other words, a person has no share in the deeds of others apart from that which is gifted to him, at which point it is for him. As for his words ﷺ: {No one fasts on behalf of someone else, and no one prays on behalf of someone else.}, this has to do with discharging one's responsibility,[8] not reward. If someone prays, fasts, or gives in charity and then dedicates the reward to someone else, whether living or dead, it is permissible and the reward reaches them according to Muslim Orthodoxy, and the same is found in *al-Badāʾiʿ*.[9] This is how we know that there is no difference between dedicating the reward to the deceased or to the living, and the apparent purport is that there is no difference between intending that the reward for the deed be for someone else while doing it and doing the deed for oneself and then dedicating the reward to someone else afterwards, because his words are not qualified.'[10]

Imam al-Mawṣalī says in the book *al-Ikhtiyār*:

'The position of Muslim Orthodoxy is that a person may dedicate the reward of his deed to someone else and it will reach that person. This is due to the ḥadīth of the Khathʿamī woman,[11] which was quoted in the chapter on the Ḥajj, and due to what has been related in which he ﷺ sacrificed two black and white rams, one for himself and the other on behalf of

8 (tn): i.e. one is not allowed to abandon praying or fasting and have someone else do these deeds on his behalf.

9 (tn): i.e. *Badāʾiʿ as-Ṣanāʾiʿ fī Tartīb ash-Sharāʾiʿ* by ʿAlāʾ ad-Dīn al-Kāsānī.

10 *Al-Baḥr ar-Rāʾiq Sharḥ Kanz ad-Daqāʾiq*, 3:63, by Zayn ad-Dīn ibn Ibrāhīm ibn Muḥammad, known as Ibn Nujaym al-Maṣrī (d.970 AH).

11 (tn): i.e. a woman from the tribe of Khathʿam who asked if she might do the Ḥajj on behalf of her elderly father, and he ﷺ granted her permission.

his Ummah, i.e. he dedicated the reward to his Ummah. It has also been related that a man said, 'O Messenger of Allah, my mother has departed; will she get the reward if I give in charity on her behalf? He replied, {Yes, and you, too.} A woman lifted up her child and said, 'O Messenger of Allah, is there a Ḥajj for this one?' He replied, {Yes, and you get reward.} There are many narrations. There are those who disagree and say that the reward does not reach, and they cite the Exalted One's words: **"that man will have nothing but what he strives for"** [an-Najm 53:39]

'and his ﷺ words: {When the child of Adam dies, his deeds come to an end apart from three...}.

'There are several ways to respond to this verse. The **first** is that it is preceded by His ﷻ words:

﴿أَمْ لَمْ يُنَبَّأْ بِمَا فِي صُحُفِ مُوسَىٰ ۝٣٦ وَإِبْرَٰهِيمَ ٱلَّذِى وَفَّىٰٓ﴾

"Or has he not been informed what is in the texts of Mūsā and of Ibrāhīm, who paid his dues in full." [an-Najm 53:36-37]

'Thus, we are being informed of what the revealed laws of those two Prophets were, which means that they do not apply to us. We have related the opposite of that from our Prophet ﷺ. ʿAlī ؓ said, 'This is for the people of Ibrāhīm and Mūsā. As for this Ummah, they have what they strive for and what is striven for on their behalf'.

'The **second** is that it is abrogated by the Exalted One's statement:

﴿أَلْحَقْنَا بِهِمْ ذُرِّيَّتَهُمْ﴾

"We shall unite those who believed with their progeny..." [at-Ṭūr 52:21]

'The progeny are entered into Paradise because of the righteousness of their ancestors. This was stated by Ibn ʿAbbās.

'The **third** is what was stated by Rabīʿ ibn Anas, "What is meant by man here is the disbeliever. As for the believer, he has the reward of his striving and what is striven for on his behalf".

'The **fourth** is to understand the letter *lām*[12] to mean *ʿalā*,[13] and it is possible. For example, he fell down on his hands and on his mouth.[14] Thus, it is as if Allah is saying that there is nothing upon man apart from what he strives for, and thus he bears the weight of it. This reconciles between the verse and the ḥadīth, because it is a correct meaning regarding which there is no difference of opinion, and no specification applies to it.

'The **fifth** is that he strove to dedicate the reward for his deed to someone else, and thus he has what he strove, acting in accordance with the verse.

'The **sixth** is that striving is of different types. There is striving by way of action and by way of speaking. There is striving because of one's relatives, as well as a friend who strives because of his friendship. There are also deeds of goodness and righteousness and matters of the Religion that a person can strive to do and people love him as a result and supplicate for him, and they dedicate the reward for their deeds to him. All of that is because of his striving, and we have said this based on the verse, so it is not an evidence against us.

'As for the ḥadīth, it necessitates that one's deeds are cut off, and there is nothing to discuss in that regard. The discussion is about whether the reward for other people's deeds reaches him, and the ḥadīth does not negate that. Everyone has deemed it good, and thus it is something good, based on the ḥadīth.'[15]

---

12 (tn): which normally indicates possession, i.e. to have.
13 (tn): i.e. upon, or on.
14 Ar. *lilyadayni wa lilfam*.
15 *Al-Ikhtiyār li Taʿlīl al-Mukhtār* by al-Mawṣalī al-Ḥanafī, 4:179. (tn): The ḥadīth being referred to here is most likely: {What the Muslims see as good is good in the sight of Allah.}, which is related by ʿAbdullah ibn Masʿūd.

This has been established by the last of the verifying scholars and the axis of fatwā in the Ḥanafī School, Ibn ʿĀbidīn ash-Shāmī ﷺ in more than one place in his well-known *Ḥāshiyah*. For example:

'Our scholars have unequivocally stated in the chapter on performing the Ḥajj on behalf of others that a person may dedicate the reward for his deeds to someone else, whether that deed be a prayer, a fast, giving in charity, or something else, and the same is mentioned in *al-Hidāyah*. In the chapter on the zakāt in the book *at-Tatārkhāniyyah ʿan al-Muḥīṭ*, it states, "If one is giving in charity, it is best to intend all believing men and women, because it will reach them and their reward will not be decreased in the slightest. This is the position of Muslim Orthodoxy".'[16]

This has also been affirmed by az-Zaylaʿī in *Tabyīn al-Ḥaqāʾiq Sharḥ Kanz ad-Daqāʾiq*[17] as well as by al-Badr al-ʿAynī in his commentary on the *Kanz*, which is called *Ramz al-Ḥaqāʾiq*.

16 *Ad-Durr al-Mukhtār wa Ḥāshiyat Ibn ʿĀbidīn* (*Radd al-Muḥtār*), 2:433. In the same book, see also 1:439, 2:74, 2:425-426, and other parts.

17 See *Tabyīn al-Ḥaqāʾiq Sharḥ Kanz ad-Daqāʾiqwa Ḥāshiyat ash-Shiblī*, 2:83.

The Mālikī School

Ibn al-Ḥājj says in *al-Madkhal*:

'If one were to recite in one's house and dedicate the reward to someone else, the reward would reach that person. The way to do it is that once one has finished one's recitation, one dedicates the reward to that person, or one says, 'O Allah, grant its reward to him'. That is a supplication for reward, because it will reach one's brother, and there is no dispute that supplications reach those who are supplicated for.'[18]

Al-Qarāfī says regarding the 172nd case:

'That which is said and is not differed over is that they attain the blessings[19] of the recitation, not the reward, just as they attain the blessings of having a righteous person buried next to them and vice versa, because blessings do not depend on anything. An animal attains the blessings of the one riding it or accompanying it, and blessings are not disputed.'

Then he says:

'As for this issue, even though it is differed over, a person should not neglect it. Maybe it is true that it will reach the deceased; it is a matter of the unseen for us. There is no difference of opinion over the ruling in the Revealed Law. Rather it is over whether it actually happens or not. The same applies to the *tahlīl*[20] that people usually do nowadays; it should be done,

18 *Al-Madkhal* by Ibn al-Ḥājj, 1:266.
19 Ar. *al-barakah*.
20 (tn): i.e. to say *Lā ilāha ill Allāh*.

and in doing do so they should rely on Allah the Exalted's grace and what He facilitates. Allah's grace should be sought by every means possible, and from Allah comes munificence and beneficence. This is what befits the slave.'[21]

In his commentary on *Ṣaḥīḥ Muslim*, when commenting on the ḥadīth of the palm-leaf stalk[22] in which the Prophet ﷺ placed it on two graves and then said:

{Maybe it will be mitigated for them until they dry.},

al-Qāḍī ʿIyāḍ says:

'Based on this, the scholars have recommended that the Qurʾān be recited over the deceased, because if the *tasbīḥ*[23] of two palm-leaf stalks mitigates what the deceased is experiencing, and they are inanimate objects, the recitation of the Qurʾān has greater reason to do so.'[24]

Shaykh Abū Zayd al-Fāsī says in the chapter on the performing the Ḥajj on behalf of others, and he was answering a question:

'The deceased benefits from the recitation of the Qurʾān. This is the correct position, and the difference of opinion therein is well-known. Receiving a wage for it is permissible, and Allah knows best.'

Al-ʿAllāmah Kanūn al-Fāsī quoted this from him.[25]

---

21 *Al-Furūq* by al-Qarāfī, which is known as *Anwār al-Burūq fī Anwāʾ al-Furūq*, 3:192.

22 Ar. *al-jarīdah*.

23 (tn): i.e. glorification, to say *Subḥān Allah*.

24 See the book *Hidāyā al-Aḥyāʾ lil Amwāt* by as-Sayyid ash-Sharīf Muḥammad ʿAlawī al-Mālikī ؒ.

25 See the book *Hidāyā al-Aḥyāʾ lil Amwāt* by as-Sayyid ash-Sharīf Muḥammad ʿAlawī al-Mālikī ؒ

The Shāfiʿī School

Imam an-Nawawī 🝡 says:

'Our companions 🝡 have said that it is recommended for the visitor to give greetings of peace over the graves and to supplicate for the person he is visiting as well as everyone else in the graveyard. It is best to say the greeting of peace and the supplications that are established in the ḥadīth. It is also recommended to recite whatever one is able to of the Qurʾān and supplicate for them afterwards. Ash-Shāfiʿī has clearly stated this and the companions agreed with him.'[26]

Shaykh al-Islām Zakariyyā al-Anṣārī says in *Sharḥ Manhaj at-Ṭullāb*:

'(And he is benefitted by), i.e. the deceased by his heirs as well as others, (charity and supplication) by consensus, as well as other deeds. As for the Exalted One's statement: **"that man will have nothing but what he strives for"** [an-Najm 53:39], it is a general statement that has specific application.[27] It has also been said that it is abrogated. Just as the deceased benefits from the aforementioned, so does the one giving the charity as well as the one supplicating. As for recitation, an-Nawawī has said in his commentary on *Muslim* that the well-known position of the Shāfiʿī school is that its reward does not reach the deceased. Some of our companions have said that it does reach, and groups of scholars have held the position that the reward for all acts of worship reaches the deceased, whether

---

26 *Al-Majmūʿ Sharḥ al-Muhadhdhib*, 5:311.

27 (tn): i.e. *ʿām makhṣūṣ*. See *al-Wajīz fī Uṣūl at-Tashrīʿ al-Islāmī* by Imam Muḥammad Ḥasan Hītū (Beirut: Muʾassasah ar-Risālah, 1436/2015), 180.

that act of worship be a prayer, a fast, a recitation, or anything else. What he said regarding the well-known position of the school is understood to apply when one recites but not in the presence of the deceased and one has not intended that the reward for the recitation go to him, or one intended such but did not supplicate. Indeed, as-Subkī has said, "What is evidenced by deriving from the reports is that if one intends to benefit a deceased person by way of a portion of the Qur'an, it will benefit him, and this is obvious". I have also mentioned this in *Sharḥ ar-Rawḍ*.'[28]

Al-Khaṭīb ash-Shirbīnī says in *Mughnī al-Muḥtāj ilā Maʿrifat Maʿānī Alfāẓ al-Minhāj*:

'In his commentary on *Muslim* and well as in *al-Adhkār*, the author[29] narrates a position that the reward for recitation reaches the deceased, as is the position of the three other Imams. A group of our companions have also chosen that position, including Ibn as-Ṣalāḥ, al-Muḥibb at-Ṭabarī, Ibn Abī ad-Damm, the author of *adh-Dhakhāʾir*, Ibn Abī ʿAsrūn, and it is what the people do; what the Muslims see as good is good in the sight of Allah. As-Subkī has said, "What is evidenced by deriving from the reports is that if one intends to benefit a deceased person by way of a portion of the Qur'an, and to mitigate what he is experiencing, it will benefit him, as it has been established that when the *Fātiḥah* is recited for someone who has been stung, it benefits him. The Prophet ﷺ affirmed this when he said: {What will make you realise that it is a *ruqyah*?} If the living can be benefitted by intending such then all the more reason that the deceased should benefit".

'Al-Qāḍī Ḥusayn deemed it permissible to hire someone to recite the Qurʾān in the presence of the deceased. Ibn as-Ṣalāḥ said, "He should say, 'O Allah, give the reward for what we have recited to so-and-so', and thus he makes it a supplication,

28 *Sharḥ Manhaj at-Ṭullāb*, 3:286. (tn): *Sharḥ ar-Rawḍ* is the book *Asnā al-Muṭālib Sharḥ Rawḍ at-Ṭālib*, which is Zakariyyā al-Anṣārī's commentary on the book *Rawḍat-Ṭālib* by Ibn al-Muqrī.

29 (tn): i.e. Imam an-Nawawī, the author of *Minhāj at-Ṭālibīn*, which is the book that al-Khaṭīb ash-Shirbīnī is commenting on.

and no one, near or far, disputes that. One should have firm resolve that the benefits reaches, because if it does, and it is permissible for one to supplicate for someone else, then there is greater reason for it to be permissible if one is supplicating for oneself. Furthermore, this is not confined to recitation. Rather, it applies to all deeds".'[30]

Ibn Shihāb ar-Ramlī says in *Nihāyat al-Muḥtāj*:

'Regarding recitation, there is one position, which is that of the three other Imams, and it is that its reward reaches the deceased merely by intending such, and this has been adopted by many of our imams. A group of scholars hold that the initial position of the school applies to one's recitation when not in the presence of the deceased and when the one reciting does not intend to dedicate the reward for his recitation to him, or he does intend such but does not supplicate. 'Ibn as-Ṣalāḥ said, "One should have firm resolve that the benefits reaches: O Allah, give the reward for what we have recited – i.e. the same reward, this is what is meant, even if one does say so unequivocally – to so-and-so', because if supplication can benefit other than the one supplicating, there is greater reason for supplication to benefit when one supplicates for oneself, and this applies to all deeds".'[31]

30 *Mughnī al-Muḥtāj ilā Maʿrifat Maʿānī Alfāẓ al-Minhāj*, 4:110.
31 *Nihāyat al-Muḥtāj ilā Sharḥ al-Minhāj*, 6:93.

The Ḥanbalī School

Īmam Aḥmad ibn Ḥanbal ﷺ said:

'Every act of goodness reaches the deceased, because of the texts that have been transmitted on the matter.'

Similar statements are found in the books of the school.[32]

Al-Muwaffaq ibn Qudāmah al-Maqdisī al-Ḥanbalī says in the book *al-Mughnī*:

'Section: Any act of worship that a person does and dedicates its reward to a deceased Muslim, the deceased benefits, if Allah so wills. As for supplication, seeking forgiveness, giving in charity, and carrying out obligations, I know of no difference of opinion therein. The obligations may be performed by proxy, and Allah the Exalted has said:

32 For example:
Al-Furūʿ by Muḥammad ibn Mufliḥ ibn Muḥammad ibn Mufarraj, or ʿAbdullah, Shams ad-Dīn al-Maqdisī, then as-Ṣāliḥī, al-Ḥanbalī, 3:423.
Al-Mubdiʿ fi Sharḥ al-Muqniʿ by Ibrāhīm ibn Muḥammad ibn ʿAbdillāh ibn Muḥammad ibn Mufliḥ, 2:281.
Daqāʾiq Uwli an-Nuhā li Sharḥ al-Muntahā, famously known as *Sharḥ Muntahā al-Irādāt*, 1:385.
Kashshāf al-Qināʿ ʿan Matn al-Iqnāʿ, both by Manṣūr ibn Yūnus ibn Ṣalāḥ ad-Dīn ibn Ḥusayn ibn Idrīs al-Buhūtī al-Ḥanbalī, d. 1051 AH, 2:147.
Muṭālib Uwlī an-Nuhā fi Sharḥ Ghāyat al-Muntahā by Muṣṭafā ibn Saʿd ibn ʿAbduh, known as as-Suyūtī, called ar-Ruḥaybānī on account of where he was born and then ad-Dimashqī, al-Ḥanbalī, d. 1243 AH, 1:936.
Ar-Rawḍ al-Murbiʿ by Manṣūr ibn Yūnus ibn Ṣalāḥ ad-Dīn ibn Ḥusayn ibn Idrīs al-Buhūtī al-Ḥanbalī with the supercommentary of ʿAbdur Raḥmān ibn Muḥammad ibn Qāsim al-ʿĀṣimī al-Ḥanbalī an-Najdī, d.1392 AH, 3:139.

﴿وَٱلَّذِينَ جَآءُو مِنۢ بَعْدِهِمْ يَقُولُونَ رَبَّنَا ٱغْفِرْ لَنَا وَلِإِخْوَٰنِنَا ٱلَّذِينَ سَبَقُونَا بِٱلْإِيمَـٰنِ﴾

"Those who came after them say, 'Our Lord, forgive us and our brothers who preceded in faith..." [al-Ḥashr 59:10]

'Allah the Exalted has also said:

﴿وَٱسْتَغْفِرْ لِذَنۢبِكَ وَلِلْمُؤْمِنِينَ وَٱلْمُؤْمِنَـٰتِ﴾

"...and ask forgiveness for your sin, and for the believing men and women." [Muḥammad 47:19]

'And the Prophet ﷺ supplicated for Abū Salamah when he died, and the deceased person that he prayed over in the ḥadīth of ʿAwf ibn Mālik, and for every deceased person that he prayed over. He also supplicated for Dhūl Bajādayn until he had buried him. Allah has legislated that for anyone who prays over a deceased person. A man asked the Prophet ﷺ and said, 'O Messenger of Allah, my mother has passed away. If I give charity on her behalf, will it benefit her?' He replied, {Yes.} This was related by Abū Dāwūd, and it was related from Saʿd ibn ʿUbādah.

'A woman came to the Prophet ﷺ and said, 'O Messenger of Allah ﷺ, Allah has made the Ḥajj an obligation and my father is now an old man. He cannot stay fast on a mount. May I do the Ḥajj on his behalf?' He replied, {If your father had a debt, would you pay it off?} She said, 'Yes'. He said, {Allah's debt has more right to be paid off.} He said to the one who asked him, 'My mother has died and she owed a month of fasting. Should I fast on her behalf?' He replied, {Yes.}.

'These ḥadīths are authentic, and they evidence that the deceased benefits from all acts of worship, because fasting, the Ḥajj, supplication, and seeking forgiveness are all physical acts of worship. Allah causes their benefit to reach the deceased, and the same goes for other acts of worship, along with the ḥadīth we mentioned regarding the reward for whoever recites Yā Sīn, and that by its recitation, Allah the Exalted mitigates what the people of the graves are experiencing. ʿAmr ibn al-ʿĀṣ has related, {If your father is a Muslim, emancipate a slave on his behalf, or give in charity on his behalf, or do the Ḥajj on his behalf. That will reach him.} This is general; it applies to a voluntary Ḥajj and other matters, because it is a deed of righteousness and obedience, and thus its benefit and reward reach, just like charity, fasting, and the obligatory Ḥajj.

'And this is how the legitimacy of this matter according to the Four Schools is made clear to us.

'Ash-Shāfiʿī said,

"Apart from what is obligatory, charity, supplication, and seeking forgiveness, nothing is done for the benefit of the deceased, and its reward does not reach him. This is due to the Exalted One's words: **"that man will have nothing but what he strives for"** [an-Najm 53:39] and his ﷺ words: {When the son of Adam dies, his deeds come to an end apart from three: ongoing charity, knowledge that is benefited from after him, or a righteous child that supplicates for him.} Because the benefit does not go further than the doer, the reward, likewise, does not go further".

'One of them said, "If the Qurʾān is recited in the presence of the deceased, or its reward is gifted to him, the reward is for the reciter, and the deceased is treated as if he were present, and thus it is hoped that he will be shown mercy. And we have what we have mentioned, and it is the consensus of the Muslims, for in every time and place they gather and recite the Qurʾān and gift its reward to their deceased, without any objection. It is also because of the authentic ḥadīth in which the Prophet ﷺ said: {The deceased is punished by his family weeping over him}, and Allah's magnanimity is above letting the punishment for disobedience reach him while blocking reward".

'It is also because the One conveying the reward for what they have approved is capable of conveying the reward for what they have denied, and the verse is confined to what they have approved. What we have differed over has the same meaning, and thus we use it to make an analogy. They have no argument in the report that they have cited, as it only evidences that one's actions have come to an end. It does not evidence that.[33] If it did evidence that, it would be confined to what they have approved, as well as what has the same meaning, which they have denied, and thus it would also be confined to the results of making an analogy. What they have mentioned by way of meaning is not correct, because the reward going further than the doer is not a branch of the benefit going further. Then it is baseless regarding fasting and the Ḥajj. It has no foundation worthy of consideration, and Allah knows best'.[34]

33 (tn): i.e. it does not evidence that reward and benefit have come to an end.

34 *Al-Mughnī* by Ibn Qudāmah, 2:423.

Mentioning Some of the Evidences for the Legitimacy of This Matter

We have already seen many of the evidences in the fiqh books from the Four Schools that we have just cited, just as we have seen the refutation of what those who disagree cite as evidence and how the doubts that they stir up in this matter are to be answered.

We shall mention them here separately so that whoever wants to can refer to them:[35]

It is on the authority of our master Maʿqal ibn Yasār ﵁ that the Messenger of Allah ﷺ said:

{Yā Sīn is the heart of the Qurʾān; no one recites it seeking Allah and the abode of the Hereafter except that Allah forgives him. Recite it over your deceased.[36]}[37]

What is meant by '*mawtākum*' is those who are actually dead, not those who are approaching death. Ash-Shawkānī said, as well as al-Muḥibb at-Ṭabarī in explaining the meaning of *mawtākum* in the ḥadīth, 'The word means those who are

---

35 Taken from the book *al-Mawsūʿah al-Yūsufiyyah* by Shaykh Yūsuf Khaṭṭār.

36 Ar. *mawtākum*.

37 Collected by Abū Dāwūd (3121), Ibn Mājah (1448), an-Nasāʾī in the chapter on the daily and nightly deeds (1074), Aḥmad (5;26), al-Ḥākim (1;565), al-Baghawī (1464), Ibn Abī Shaybah (3:237), at-Ṭabarānī in *al-Kabīr* (20, no.510), al-Bayhaqī (3/383), as-Suyūṭī mentioned it in *al-Jāmiʿ as-Ṣaghīr* (1344) and indicated that it was *ḥasan*, at-Ṭayālasī (931), and Ibn Ḥibbān (3002). It is on the authority of Abū Hurayrah and Abū Dharr al-Ghifārī, who said that the Messenger of Allah ﷺ said: {There is no one who dies and Yā Sīn is read in his presence except that Allah ﷻ makes it easy for him.} This was collected by ad-Daylamī (6099).

dead, and it metaphorically includes those who are approaching death, and it cannot result in such[38] unless the context indicates it.'[39]

When there is no context to indicate such, the word is understood according to its literal meaning and does not become metaphorical, that is, interpreting the word *mawtākum* in the ḥadīth to mean those who are approaching death. This is because there is no context to indicate such, and thus the meaning of *mawtākum* remains those who are actually dead. And we know that the dead are only those who are alive in their graves; they hear our recitation and our supplication. We have already covered this in detail in the chapter on *tawassul* and *istighāthah*, at the beginning of the section on *tawassul* with the dead (*al-muntaqilīn*), so one can refer to that.

It is on the authority of ʿAbdur Raḥmān ibn al-ʿAlāʾ ibn al-Ḥajjāj, from his father, and he said, 'My father, al-Ḥajjāj, said to me, "My dear son, when I die, dig a *laḥd*[40] for me and when you have placed me in my *laḥd*, say *Bismillāh wa ʿala Millati Rasūl Illāh.*[41] Then pour the soil on top of me. Then, by my head, read the opening and closing verses of al-Baqarah, for indeed I heard the Messenger of Allah ﷺ saying that".'[42]

Some people have said that this ḥadīth is *mursal*[43] and if we submit that it is *mursal*, the majority of *fuqahāʾ* and scholars of *uṣūl al-fiqh* say that a *mursal* ḥadīth may be cited as evidence.

38 (tn): i.e. to mean 'dying' and not 'dead'.
39 *Nayl al-Awṭār*, 3:25.
40 (tn): i.e. a grave in which the corpse is placed inside a lateral niche that is dug out of the bottom of the side that faces the *qiblah*.
41 (tn): i.e. In the Name of Allah, and upon the way of Allah's Messenger.
42 Collected by at-Ṭabarānī in *al-Kabīr* (13:136), and al-Haythamī mentioned it in *Majmaʿ az-Zawaʾid* (2442) and said that the men in its chain of transmission are reliable.
43 (tn): According to the scholars of ḥadīth, *mursal* means that the Companion has been omitted from the chain of transmission. According to the scholars of *uṣūl al-fiqh*, it means that a narrator has been omitted, wherever in the chain that may be. (*al-Fatḥ al-Mubīn bi Sharḥ al-Arbaʿīn*, p.522.)

Ibn Kathīr says in his book *al-Bāʾith al-Ḥathīth*, 'Ibn aṣ-Ṣalāḥ says that citing the *mursal* as evidence is the position of Mālik and Abū Ḥanīfah and their followers. I – i.e. Ibn Kathīr – say that it is reported from Imam Aḥmad ibn Ḥanbal in one narration'.[44]

Their statement that the ḥadīth is *mursal* is rejected because the ḥadīth's chain of transmission is uninterrupted,[45] and it is: at-Ṭabarānī said, 'al-Ḥusayn ibn Isḥāq at-Tastarī related to me, "ʿAlī ibn Ḥujr related to us, 'Mubashshir ibn Ismāʿīl related to us, "ʿAbdur Raḥmān ibn al-ʿAlāʾ ibn al-Ḥajjāj related to me from his father, 'My father, al-Ḥajjāj Abū Khālid said, "My dear son, when I die..."'"'"'[46]

Al-Ḥāfiẓ as-Suyūṭī has collected, as well as Abū al-Qāsim in his *Qawāʾid*:

{Whoever enters the graveyard and then recites the Fātiḥah, *Alhākum at-Takāthur*,[47] and *Qul Huw Allāhu Aḥad*[48] and then says, 'I dedicate the reward for what I have recited of Your Speech to the believing men and women in their graves', they[49] will be intercessors for him on the Day of Standing.}

It is on the authority of our master Ibn ʿUmar ﷺ that after the burial, it is recommended to read the opening verses and closing verses of Sūrat al-Baqarah.[50]

It is on the authority of our master Abū ad-Dardāʾ ﷺ:

{There is no dying person who has Yā Sīn read next to his head except that Allah makes the matter easy for him.}[51]

---

44 *Al-Bāʿith al-Ḥathīth fī Muṣṭalaḥ al-Ḥadīth*, 48.
45 Ar. *muttaṣil.*
46 *Ar-Radd al-Muḥkam al-Matīn* by Shaykh ʿAbdullah as-Ṣiddīq, 283, and *Naṣb ar-Rāyah* by az-Zaylaʿī, 2:302.
47 (tn): i.e. Sūrat at-Takāthur (102).
48 (tn): i.e. Sūrat al-Ikhlāṣ (112).
49 (tn): i.e. those believing men and women.
50 *Al-Adhkār* by an-Nawawī, 123.
51 Ad-Daylamī (6099).

It is on the authority of Abū ash-Shaʿthāʾ, the companion of Ibn ʿAbbās, that it is recommended to recite Sūrat ar-Raʿd and that it mitigates what the deceased is experiencing. Furthermore, it is on the authority of ash-Shaʿbī, who said, 'The Helpers[52] would recommend that Sūrat al-Baqarah be recited in the presence of the deceased'.[53]

It is on the authority of Imam Aḥmad, who said, 'Al-Mughīrah narrated to us, "Ṣafwān narrated to us, and said, 'The shaykhs would say, "If it is read – i.e. Yā Sīn – on behalf of the deceased, what he is experiencing is mitigated".'"'

52 Ar. *Al-Anṣār*.

53 This was quoted by ash-Shawkānī in *Nayl al-Awṭār*, 3:25, and is also mentioned in *Subul as-Salām*, 2:91.

Some Clear Texts That Demonstrate the Legitimacy of This Matter from Imams Who Are Relied upon by Those Who Hold a Different View & Attribute Themselves to Them

The author of *al-Futūḥāt Al-Ilāhiyyah ʿan Tafsīr al-Jalālayn,* in commenting on Allah the Exalted's words **"that man will have nothing but what he strives for"** [an-Najm 53:39], quotes from Shaykh Ibn Taymiyyah more than twenty ways in which the Muslim benefits from the deeds of others. He says,

'Shaykh Taqī ad-Dīn Abū al-ʿAbbās ibn Taymiyyah says,

"Whoever believes that a person only benefits from his own deeds has violated the consensus, and it is baseless from numerous angles:

"The **first** is that a person benefits from someone else's supplication, which means he benefits from someone else's deed.

"The **second** is that the Prophet intercedes for the people standing for the Reckoning, then for the people of Paradise for them to enter it, and then for the people of major sins to exit the Fire, and this is benefitting from someone else's deed.

"The **third** is that every Prophet and righteous person has an intercession, which is benefitting from someone else's deed.

"The **fourth** is that the angels supplicate and seek forgiveness for those on Earth, and this is an example of people's benefitting from the deeds of others.

"The **fifth** is that Allah the Exalted takes out of the Fire those who have never done any good deed purely out of His mercy, and thus they benefit and it has nothing to do with their deeds.

"The **sixth** is that the children of believers enter Paradise because of the deeds of their parents, and thus they benefit purely from the deeds of others.

"The **seventh** is what Allah the Exalted says regarding the two young orphans:

﴿وَكَانَ أَبُوهُمَا صَـٰلِحًا﴾

"Their father was one of the righteous." [al-Kahf 18:82]

"The two of them thus benefitted from the righteousness of their father, and he has nothing to do with their striving.

"The **eighth** is that the deceased benefits from charity on his behalf as well as emancipation, based on the text of the Sunnah and consensus. These are someone else's deeds.

"The **ninth** is that the obligatory Ḥajj is lifted from the deceased if his guardian[54] does it for him, based on the text of the Sunnah. This is benefitting from someone else's deed.

"The **tenth** is that the vowed Ḥajj and the vowed fast are lifted from the deceased if someone else does it, based on the text of the Sunnah. This is benefitting from someone else's deed.

"The **eleventh** is the debtor whom he ﷺ forbade praying over until Abū Qatādah had paid off his debt. Furthermore, ʿAlī ibn Abī Ṭālib paid off someone else's debt. Each benefited from the Prophet's ﷺ prayer over him and his skin was cooled because his debt was paid off, which was someone else's deed.

54 Ar. *walī*, which means any of the deceased's relatives.

"The **twelfth** is that the Prophet ﷺ said regarding someone who was praying by himself: {Is there anyone who might be charitable towards this person and pray with him?}[55] He thus attained the credit of praying in congregation because of someone else's action.

"The **thirteenth** is that a person can be absolved of the creation's debts if a judge gives such a verdict, and this is an example of benefitting from someone else's deed.

"The **fourteenth** is that if a person has responsibilities and misdeeds and he is exonerated of them, they are lifted from him, and this is an example of benefitting from someone else's deed.

"The **fifteenth** is that the righteous neighbour benefits others when he is among the living and when he is among the dead; reports regarding such have reached us. This is another example of benefitting from someone else's deed.

"The **sixteenth** is that the person who sits with the people of *dhikr* is shown mercy because of them, even though he is not one of them, did not sit with them for that reason but for some other need, and actions are only by intentions. He benefits from the deeds of others.

"The **seventeenth** is that praying over the deceased and supplicating for him in the prayer means that the deceased benefits from the prayer of the living, which is someone else's deed.

"The **eighteenth** is that the Friday Prayer depends on a certain number of people coming together, and the same goes for congregational prayers, and thus people benefit from one another.

"The **nineteenth** is that Allah said to His Prophet ﷺ:

55 Collected by Aḥmad (3:5), at-Tirmidhī (220), Abū Dāwūd (574), ad-Dārimī (1341), Abū Yaʿlā (1057), and al-Ḥākim (1:109), who declared it authentic and adh-Dhahabī agreed with him.

﴿وَمَا كَانَ ٱللَّهُ لِيُعَذِّبَهُمْ وَأَنتَ فِيهِمْ﴾

"Allah would not punish them while you were among them." [al-Anfāl 8:33]

"The Exalted One has also said:

﴿وَلَوْلَا رِجَالٌ مُّؤْمِنُونَ وَنِسَآءٌ مُّؤْمِنَـٰتٌ﴾

"...had it not been for some men and women who are believers..." [al-Fatḥ 48:25] and

﴿وَلَوْلَا دَفْعُ ٱللَّهِ ٱلنَّاسَ بَعْضَهُم بِبَعْضٍ﴾

"If it were not for Allah's driving some people back by means of others..." [al-Baqarah 2:251]

"Allah the Exalted thus drove punishment back from some people because of some other people, and this is another example of people's benefitting from the deeds of others.

"The **twentieth** is that zakāt al-fiṭr is obligatory upon the small child and other people that a man provides for, and thus they benefit because he pays it on their behalf while they do not strive at all.

"The **twenty-first** is that zakāt must be paid on children's wealth and that of the insane, and they are rewarded for its being paid and they do not have to strive. Whoever thinks over what he knows will find that a person can benefit from that which he has not done in countless ways, so how can it be permissible to interpret the verse in a way that contradicts the unequivocal Book and Sunnah, the consensus of the Ummah, and the general understanding of what is meant by 'man'?'"[56]

56 Quoted from the book *Fawāʾid wa Manāfiʿ wa Nafāʾis* by the ʿAllāmah, the Faqīh, Shaykh Muḥammad Hāshim al-Majdhūb ar-Rifāʿī al-Ḥusaynī, may Allah preserve him.

After quoting one of Imam Aḥmad's positions on recitation over the grave and that he gave a dispensation therein because it had reached him that Ibn ʿUmar had requested that the opening and closing verses of al-Baqarah be recited at his grave, and that reciting Sūrat al-Baqarah had been narrated from some Companions, Ibn Taymiyyah also says in *al-Fatāwā al-Kubrā*:

'Reciting at the time of burial has been transmitted in general. As for afterwards, no report has been transmitted, and Allah knows best.'[57]

Shaykh Ibn al-Qayyim ﵀ says in the book *ar-Rūḥ*:

'It has been quoted from a group of the First Three Generations[58] that they would request that the Qurʾān be recited over their graves at the time of burial. ʿAbdul Ḥaqq has said, "It is related that ʿAbdullah ibn ʿUmar commanded that Sūrat al-Baqarah be read at his grave. Among those who saw that is al-Maʿlā ibn ʿAbdur Raḥmān. Imam Aḥmad denied that at first as no report had reached it. Then he went back on his position".

'Al-Khallāl says in the book *al-Jāmiʿ*, in the chapter on reciting at graves, "Al-ʿAbbās ibn Muḥammad ad-Dūrī has narrated to us, 'Yaḥyā ibn Muʿīn has narrated to us, "Mubashshir al-Ḥalabī has narrated to us, "ʿAbdur Raḥmān ibn al-ʿAlāʾ ibn al-Ḥajjāj narrated to me from his father and said, "My father said, 'When I die, put me in my *laḥd* and say *Bismillāh wa ʿala Sunnati Rasūl Illāh.*[59] Then pour the soil on top of me and, read the opening verses of al-Baqarah by my head, for indeed I heard ʿAbdullah ibn ʿUmar saying that'."'""

"ʿAbbās ad-Dūrī said, "I asked Aḥmad ibn Ḥanbal. I said, 'Have you memorised anything regarding reciting over the grave?' He said, 'No'. I asked Yaḥyā ibn Muʿīn and he narrated this ḥadīth to me".

57 *Al-Fatāwā al-Kubrā* by Ibn Taymiyyah, 3:25.

58 Ar. *as-Salaf.*

59 (tn): i.e. In the Name of Allah, and upon the Sunnah of Allah's Messenger.

'Al-Khallāl said, "And al-Ḥasan ibn Aḥmad al-Warrāq narrated to me, "ʿAlī ibn Mūsā al-Ḥaddād narrated to me, and he was thoroughly veracious,[60] and said, "I was with Aḥmad ibn Ḥanbal and Muḥammad ibn Qudāmah al-Jawharī at a funeral. When the deceased had been buried, a blind man sat down and started reciting at the grave. Aḥmad said to him, 'Hey you! Reciting at the grave is an innovation'. When we had left the graveyard, Muḥammad ibn Qudāmah said to Aḥmad ibn Ḥanbal, 'O Abūʿ Abdillāh, what do you say about Mubashshir al-Ḥalabī?' He replied, 'He is trustworthy'.[61] He[62] said, 'I wrote something from him. Mubashshir narrated to me from ʿAbdur Raḥmān ibn al-ʿAlāʾ ibn al-Ḥajjāj from his father that he requested that, when he was buried, that the opening and closing verses of al-Baqarah be recited by his head. He[63] said, "I heard Ibn ʿUmar requesting that"'. Aḥmad then said, 'I go back on my position. Tell the man to read'.""'

'Al-Ḥasan ibn as-Ṣabbāḥ az-Zaʿfarānī said, "I asked ash-Shāfiʿī about reciting by the grave and he said, 'There is nothing wrong with it'."

'Al-Khallāl quoted ash-Shaʿbī as saying, "When one of the Helpers would die, they would frequent his grave and recite the Qurʾān by it". He also said, "Yaḥyā an-Nāqid narrated to me and said, 'I heard al-Ḥasan ibn al-Jarawī saying, "I passed by the grave of one of my sisters and I read *Tabārak*[64] because of what has been mentioned about it. Then a man came to me and said, 'I saw your sister in my sleep and she was saying, "May Allah reward Abū ʿAlī with goodness, for I have benefitted from what he recited".'"'"'

'Al-Ḥasan ibn al-Haytham narrated to me and said, "I heard Abū Bakr ibn al-Aṭrūsh ibn Bint Abī Naṣr ibn at-Tammār saying, 'A man would come to his mother's grave on Fridays and recite Sūrat Yā Sīn. On one of those Fridays, he came and

60 Ar. *ṣadūq*.
61 Ar. *thiqah*.
62 (tn): i.e. Muḥammad ibn Qudāmah.
63 (tn): i.e. the father.
64 (tn): i.e. Sūrat al-Mulk (67).

recited Sūrat Yā Sīn and then said, "O Allah, if you have divided the reward for this sūrah, give it to the people of this graveyard". The following Friday, a woman came to him and said, "Are you so-and-so, the son of such-and-such lady?" He replied, "Yes". She then said, "One of my daughters died and in my sleep I saw her sitting on the edge of her grave, so I said, 'Why are you sitting here?' She replied that so-and-so the son of such-and-such lady came to his mother's grave, recited Sūrat Yā Sīn, and dedicated the reward to the people of the grave and that they received the solace of that, or they were forgiven, or something similar".

'In an-Nasāʾī and other collections, there is the ḥadīth of Maʿqal ibn Yasār al-Muzanī in which the Prophet ﷺ said: {Recite Yā Sīn in the presence of your deceased.[65]} It is possible that what is meant here is reciting it over the one who is approaching death, similar to his words: {Dictate *Lā ilāha ill Allāh* to your dying.[66]} It is also possible that the meaning is to recite it at the grave. The former is clearer, and for several reasons:

'The **first** is that it is very similar to {Dictate *Lā ilāha ill Allāh* to your dying.}.

'The **second** is that the one approaching death benefits from this sūrah because it mentions Allah's Oneness[67] and the Hereafter, it contains the glad tidings of Paradise for the people of *tawḥīd,* and it describes the rapture of those who die upon it. This is when Allah says:

﴿يَـٰلَيْتَ قَوْمِى يَعْلَمُونَ ۝٢٦ بِمَا غَفَرَ لِى رَبِّى وَجَعَلَنِى مِنَ ٱلْمُكْرَمِينَ﴾

"He was told, 'Enter Paradise!' He said, 'If only my people knew how my Lord has forgiven me and placed me among the honoured ones!'" [Yā Sīn 36:26-27]

---

65 Ar. *mawtākum.*

66 Ar. *mawtākum.*

67 Ar. *at-tawḥīd.*

'The spirit is given glad tidings of this, and thus it loves to meet Allah and Allah loves to meet it. This sūrah is the heart of the Qur'ān and it has an amazing quality when it is recited in the presence of someone who is dying.

'Abū al-Faraj ibn al-Jawzī said, "We were with our shaykh, Abū al-Waqt ʿAbd al-Awwal, and he was approaching death. It was the last time we saw him. He looked towards the sky, smiled, and said, **"'If only my people knew how my Lord has forgiven me and placed me among the honoured ones!"** [Yā Sīn 36:26-27] Then he died.

'The **third** is that this action is a custom of the people, from olden times through to the present; they recite Yā Sīn in the presence of their dying.

'The **fourth** is that if the Companions had understood his ﷺ words: {Recite Yā Sīn in the presence of *mawtākum*} to mean reciting it at the grave, they would not have failed to fulfil that command, and the matter would be something customary and well-known amongst them.

'The **fifth** is that benefitting from listening to it and having presence of heart and mind when it is recited just before one leaves this world is the objective. As for reciting it over the grave, there is no reward in that, because the reward is either because of reciting or because of listening, and it is a deed, and the deeds of the deceased have come to an end.

'The Ḥāfiẓ, Abū Muḥammad ʿAbdul Ḥaqq al-Ishbīlī expounded on this and said, "Mentioning what has reached us regarding the dead's asking about the living and knowing what they are saying and doing".[68] He then said, "Abū ʿUmar ibn ʿAbdul Barr mentioned the ḥadīth of Ibn ʿAbbās in which the Prophet ﷺ said: {There is no one who passes by the grave of his believing brother whom he knew in this life and gives him the greeting of peace except that he knows who it is and he returns the greeting of peace.} This is also narrated from

68 (tn): i.e. this is the title of a chapter or section.

a ḥadīth of Abū Hurayrah *marfūʿan*.[69] He[70] said, 'If he does not know him and he gives him the greeting of peace, he returns the greeting of peace'." He said, "And it is related from the ḥadīth of ʿĀʾishah ﷺ that she said, 'The Messenger of Allah ﷺ said, {There is no man who visits his brother's grave and sits over it except that he listens and responds to him until he gets up.}'"

'In this chapter, al-Ḥāfiẓ Abū Muḥammad cites as proof what Abū Dāwūd has related in his *Sunan* from the ḥadīth of Abū Hurayrah, who said, "The Messenger of Allah ﷺ said, {There is no one who gives me the greeting of peace except that Allah returns my spirit to me so I might return the greeting of peace.}" He said, "And Sulaymān ibn Nuʿaym said, 'I saw the Prophet ﷺ in my sleep and I said, "O Messenger of Allah, these people who come to you and give you the greeting of peace, are you aware of who they are?" He replied, "Yes, and I return the greeting to them".'" He said, "And he ﷺ would teach them to say upon entering a graveyard: {Peace be upon you, O people of the abode...}" Then he said, "This shows that the deceased knows who is giving him the greeting of peace and who is supplicating for him".

'Abū Muḥammad then says, "It is mentioned from al-Faḍl ibn al-Muwaffaq, who said, 'I would visit my father's grave time and again, and then I started going more often. One day, I witnessed a funeral at the graveyard in which he is buried and I was in a rush and so I was not able to visit him. That night, I saw him in my sleep and he said to me, "My dear son, why didn't you visit me?" I replied, "My dear father, you know when I visit you?" He said, "Yes, by Allah, my dear son! I watch you from the moment you emerge from the archway until you reach me, and then you sit next to me. Then you get up and I watch you until you have gone back through the archway".'"

69 (tn): i.e. a ḥadīth is that which is attributed to the Prophet ﷺ.
70 (tn): i.e. Abū Hurayrah.

'Ibn Abī ad-Dunyā said, "Ibrāhīm ibn Bashshār al-Kūfī narrated to me and said, 'Al-Faḍl ibn al-Muwaffaq narrated the same story to me'."

'It has been authentically narrated from ʿAmr ibn Dīnār that he said, "There is no one who dies except that he knows what his family are doing after him, and that they are washing him and shrouding him. He watches them".

'And it has been authentically narrated from Mujāhid that he said, "The man in his grave is given the good news of the righteousness of his child after him".'[71]

Ibn Abī ʿIzz al-Ḥanafī says in his commentary on *al-ʿAqīdah at-Ṭaḥāwiyyah:*

'By mentioning that the reward for fasting reaches, the Lawgiver has informed that the reward for recitation and similar physical acts of worship also reach.

'It has been made clear that fasting means to restrain oneself from that which breaks the fast accompanied by the intention, and the Lawgiver has unequivocally stated that its reward reaches the deceased, so imagine how much more it would be for recitation, which is an action[72] as well as an intention.

'Regarding the verse that they cite as evidence, i.e. **"that man will have nothing but what he strives for"** [an-Najm 53:39], the scholars have responded in several ways. The best responses are the following two:

'The **first** of them is that when man strives and treats others well, he gains friends, gets married, and has children. He does good to others and shows people love. They, in return, ask Allah to have mercy on him, and dedicate the reward for their good deeds to him. All of this is the result of his striving. In-

71 *Ar-Rūḥ*, 10.

72 (tn): i.e. as opposed to refraining from action, which is what fasting is.

deed, a Muslim's entering Islam with all the other Muslims is one of the greatest means by which the benefit of every Muslim reaches the person who brought that individual to Islam, during his life and after his death, and then whoever enters Islam after them.

'It has also been made clear that Allah the Exalted has made faith a means of benefitting the person who bears it because his believing brethren supplicate and strive. If he does likewise, he thus strives and partakes in the means by which that benefit reaches him.

'The **second** – which is stronger – is that the Qurʾān has not negated that a man *benefits* from the striving of others. Rather, it has negated that he *owns* the striving of others, and there is an obvious difference between the two. The Exalted One has told us that a person only owns what he strives for, and everyone else owns what he has striven for. If one wants, one may grant it to someone else, and if one wants, one may keep it for oneself.

'The Glorified One has said:

﴿أَلَّا تَزِرُ وَازِرَةٌ وِزْرَ أُخْرَىٰ ۝٣٨ وَأَن لَّيْسَ لِلْإِنسَـٰنِ إِلَّا مَا سَعَىٰ﴾

"that no burden-bearer can bear another's burden; that man will have nothing but what he strives for." [an-Najm 53:38-39]

These two verses contain clear judgements[73] and they necessitate the Exalted Lord's justice.

'The former necessitates that He not punish anyone for someone else's crime, and that He not take him to task for someone's else misdeed, unlike what earthly kings and rulers do.

73 Ar. *muḥkam*.

'The second necessitates that no one succeed except by his own deeds, so that any desire to succeed via the deeds of others is cut short. The Exalted One has said:

﴿فَٱلْيَوْمَ لَا تُظْلَمُ نَفْسٌ شَيْـًٔا وَلَا تُجْزَوْنَ إِلَّا مَا كُنتُمْ تَعْمَلُونَ﴾

"Today no soul will be wronged in any way. You will only be repaid for what you did." [Yā Sīn 36:54]

'As for citing as evidence the ḥadīth in which he ﷺ said: {When the child of Adam dies, his deeds come to an end...}, it misses the mark. He ﷺ did not say that his benefitting comes to an end. He only said that his deeds come to an end. As for someone else's deeds, they are someone else's. If one gifts it to someone else, the reward for the doer's deed reaches him, but not the reward for his actual deed. It is like someone who pays off someone's else debt; that person's debt is cleared but he does not get the reward for paying off the debt.

'As for those who make a distinction between physical and financial acts of worship, the Prophet ﷺ legislated fasting on behalf of the deceased, even though fasting may not be done vicariously.[74] Likewise, there is the ḥadīth of Jābir ؓ, who said, "I prayed the Eid al-Aḍḥā prayer with the Messenger of Allah ﷺ. When he had finished, a ram was brought and he slaughtered it. He then said: {In the Name of Allah, Allah is greater.[75] O Allah, this is for me and for those from my Ummah who have not sacrificed.}" This has been related by Aḥmad, Abū Dāwūd, and at-Tirmidhī. There is also the ḥadīth of the two rams regarding one of which he said: {O Allah, this is for my entire Ummah.}, and in another narration: {This is for Muḥammad and the Family of Muḥammad.} This was related by Aḥmad. The act of worship in sacrificing an animal is the spilling of blood, and he dedicated it to someone else.

'The Ḥajj is also a physical act of worship; money is not an integral therein but rather a means. Do you not see that

74 (tn): again, one cannot abandon fasting and have someone else do it in one's stead.

75 Ar. *Bismillāh wAllāhu Akbar*.

the Makkan must perform the Ḥajj with his body only, without money? This has been clearly stated by later followers of Abū Ḥanīfah.

'And look at the collective obligations, how one person does it on behalf of everyone else. It is because this is about dedicating reward. It is not about vicarious worship, just like an employee cannot put someone else in his place and give his wage to whomever he wants.'

Conclusion

At the end of this research, the following has been made clear.

1. Dedicating the reward for deeds is something that is legitimate, permissible, and desirable.

2. It is something that both the First Three Generations and the later generations did, as we have seen in the various ḥadīths and reports on the matter.

3. The verifying scholars of the Four Schools have clearly stated that this issue is one of consensus among the Ummah, and any position to the contrary either needs to be interpreted or is an anomaly.

4. All I can do at the end of this is turn to my Lord, the Most High, the All-Powerful, and ask Him to unite this Ummah upon the Correct Way and upon what the Greatest Beloved, the Noblest Master ﷺ was upon, as well as the excellence that the imams and scholars of the Righteous First Three Generations followed them in.

Likewise, I ask Allah to reward those partaking in this conference with the best that He has rewarded the righteous and the rightly guided imams.

Praise be to Allah, Lord of all Creation, and may Allah's prayers and peace be upon our master Muḥammad and upon all of his Family and his Companions.

Glory be to your Lord, the Lord of Might, beyond anything they describe. And peace be upon the Messengers. And praise be to Allah, the Lord of all Creation!

Appendix A

Benefitting the Deceased & Reciting the Qur'ān for Them

by Imam Jalāl ad-Dīn as-Suyūṭī[76]

Chapter 41: What Benefits the Deceased in His Grave

1262) Ibn Abī ad-Dunyā has narrated, as well as Abū Nuʿaym in *al-Ḥilyah*, from Thābit al-Bunānī, who said, 'When the believer has been placed in his grave, his righteous deeds surround him. The angel of punishment comes and one of his deeds says to him, "Get away from him. If there were no one but me, you would not get to him".'

1263) Ibn Abī ad-Dunyā has narrated from Thābit al-Bunānī, who said, 'When the righteous slave has died and been put in his grave, a bed from Paradise is brought to him and it is said to him, "Sleep. Enjoy your happiness. You have done well. Allah is pleased with you". Allah expands his grave as far as his eye can see and a door unto Paradise is opened for him. He gazes at its beauty and feels its scent. His righteous deeds surround him: fasting, prayer and piety (*birr*), and they say to him, "We tired you, made you thirsty, and kept you awake at night, and thus today we are for you wherever you want. We are lingering behind you until you arrive at your place in Paradise".'

1264) Al-Bazzār has narrated, as well as at-Ṭabarānī and al-Ḥākim, on the authority of Anas, who said, 'The Messenger of Allah ﷺ said: {Every person has three intimate friends. As for one intimate friend, he says, 'What you have spent is for you, and what you have withheld is not for you', and that is his wealth. As for another intimate friend, he says, 'I am with you. When you go to the door of the King, I leave you and go back'.

76 From the translation of *Sharḥ as-Ṣudūr bi Sharḥ Ḥāl al-Mawtā wa al-Qubūr* entitled *The Opening of the Hearts in Explaining the State of the Deceased and of the Graves* (Morrisville: The Foreword Publications, 2020), 446-463.

That is his family and his entourage. As for another intimate friend, he says, 'I am with you, wherever you enter and wherever you exit'. That is his deeds, and the person says, 'You are the least of the three to me'.}'

1265) The two Sheikhs[77] have narrated on the authority of Anas, who said, 'The Messenger of Allah ﷺ said: {When the slave dies, three follow him and then two go back while one remains. His family, his wealth and his deeds follow him, but then his family and wealth go back and his deeds remain.}'

1266) Al-Bazzār has narrated, as well as at-Ṭabarānī and al-Ḥākim, on the authority of Nuʿmān ibn Bashīr, who said, 'The Messenger of Allah ﷺ said: {The likeness of the man and the likeness of death is like a man who has three intimate friends. One of them says, 'This is my wealth. Take from it whatever you want and leave whatever you want'. Another says, 'I am with you, serving you. When you die, I will leave you'. Another says, 'I am with you. I enter with you and I exit with you, whether you are dead or alive'. As for the one who said, 'This is my wealth. Take from it whatever you want and leave whatever you want', that is his wealth. The second is his kinsfolk and the third is his deeds. They enter with him and exit with him wherever he is.}'

1267) Ibn Abī ad-Dunyā has narrated on the authority of Kaʿb, who said, 'When the righteous slave has been placed in his grave, his righteous deeds surround him: prayer, fasting, pilgrimage, *jihād* and charity. The angels of punishment come from the direction of his feet, so prayer says, "Get away from him. You have no means of getting to him. With me, he stood up at length for Allah". They then come from the direction of his head, so fasting says, "You have no means of getting to him. He thirsted at length for Allah in the abode of the world". They then come to him from the direction of his body, so pilgrimage and *jihād* say to him, "Get away from him. He wore himself out and exhausted his body, performed the pilgrimage and

77 Narrated by al-Bukhārī in the Book of Softening the Heart in the chapter on the pangs of death (Ḥadīth 6514) and narrated by Muslim in the Book of Abstinence and Softening the Heart (Ḥadīth 2960).

strived, and thus you have no means of getting to him". Then they come from the direction of his hands, so charity says, "Stay away from my companion. How much charity came from these two hands until it fell into Allah's hands, seeking Allah's countenance! Thus, you have no means of getting to him". It is then said, "Good for you! You lived well and you died well!" Then angels of mercy come and provide him with a bed from Paradise and a blanket from Paradise. His grave is expanded for him as far as his eye can see and a lamp from Paradise is brought for him, from which he seeks light until the day he is resurrected from his grave'.

1268) Ibn Abī ad-Dunyā has narrated from Yazīd ibn Abī Manṣūr that a man used to read the Qur'ān and when death came to him, the angels of punishment approached him in order to take his spirit. Then the Qur'ān came out and said, 'O Lord, I reside in the one whom You have made me reside'. He replies, 'Let the Qur'ān have its residence'.

1269) Ibn Mandah has narrated from ʿAmr ibn Murrah, who said, 'When the person has entered his grave, an angel comes to him from his left and then the Qur'ān comes and prevents him, so he says, "There is nothing between me and you. By Allah, what did he do with you?" It replies, "Was I not inside of him?" and this continues until it saves its companion'.

1270) Al-Aṣbahānī has narrated in *at-Targhīb* on the authority of Abū al-Minhāl, who said, 'The slave in his grave has no neighbour more beloved to him than a great deal of seeking forgiveness'.

1271) Al-Bukhārī has narrated in *al-Adab*, as well as Muslim, on the authority of Abū Hurayrah, who said, 'The Messenger of Allah ﷺ said: {When a person dies, his deeds come to an end except for three: ongoing charity (*ṣadaqah jāriyah*), knowledge that is benefitted from, or a righteous child that supplicates for him.}'

1272) Aḥmad[78] has narrated on the authority of Abū Umāmah from the Messenger of Allah ﷺ: {There are four who continue to be rewarded after death: the one who patrols the borders for the sake of Allah, the one who teaches knowledge, a man who gives charity, for its reward is for him as long as its active, and a man who leaves behind a righteous child who supplicates for him.}

1273) Muslim[79] has narrated on the authority Jarīr ibn ʿAbdillāh *marfūʿan*: {Whoever establishes a good practice in Islam will have its reward and the reward of whoever does it after him, without his reward being decreased in the slightest. And whoever establishes an evil practice in Islam will bear the burden of sin for it as well as the burden for whoever does it after him, without his burden being decreased in the slightest.}

1274) Ibn Saʿd has narrated on the authority of Rajāʾ ibn Ḥaywah that he said to Sulaymān ibn ʿAbdil Malik that one of the things that protect a caliph in his grave is to appoint a righteous man to succeed him.

1275) Ibn ʿAsākir has narrated from the ḥadīth of Abū Saʿīd al-Khudrī *marfūʿan*: {Whoever teaches an āyah from the Book of Allah ﷻ or a chapter of knowledge, Allah increases his reward until the Day of Standing.}

1276) Ibn Mājah[80] has narrated, as well as Ibn Khuzaymah, on the authority of Abū Hurayrah, who said, 'The Messenger of Allah ﷺ said, {Amongst the good deeds that stick to the believer after his death are knowledge that he spread, a righteous child he left behind, a *muṣḥaf* he left as an inheritance, a masjid he built, a house he built for travellers, a river he caused to flow, or charity that he extracted from his wealth while he was healthy. These will stick to him after his death.}'

---

78 Narrated by Aḥmad in his *Musnad* (5/260).

79 Narrated by Muslim in the Book of Knowledge in the chapter on whoever establishes a practices, good or evil (Ḥadīth 1017).

80 Narrated by Ibn Mājah in the introduction to the chapter on the reward of teaching people goodness.

1277) Abū Nuʿaym has narrated, as well as al-Bazzār, on the authority of Anas, who said, 'The Messenger of Allah ﷺ said, {The reward for seven things continues for the slave after he has died and is in his grave: whoever teaches knowledge, or makes a river flow, or digs a well, or plants date palms, or builds a masjid, or leaves behind a *muṣḥaf* as an inheritance, or a righteous child who seeks forgiveness for him after his death.}'

1278) At-Ṭabarānī has narrated on the authority of Thawbān that the Messenger of Allah ﷺ said: {I used to forbid you from visiting graves but now visit them, and make your visits supplications for them and seeking forgiveness for them.}

1279) Abū Nuʿaym has narrated from Ṭāwūs, who said, 'I said to my father, "What is the best thing to say in the presence of the deceased?" He replied, "Seeking forgiveness".'

1280) At-Ṭabarānī has narrated in *al-Awsaṭ*, as well as al-Bayhaqī in his *Sunan*, on the authority of Abū Hurayrah, who said, 'The Messenger of Allah ﷺ said: {Indeed Allah raises the rank of the righteous slave in Paradise, and he says, 'My Lord, how am I achieving this?' He replies, 'By way of your child seeking forgiveness for you'.}

Al-Bayhaqī's wording is: {By way of your child supplicating for you.} Al-Bukhārī has narrated it in *al-Adab* on the authority of Abū Hurayrah *mawqūfan*.

1281) He has also narrated on the authority of Abū Saʿīd al-Khudrī, who said, 'The Messenger of Allah ﷺ said: {On the Day of Standing, the man will be followed by good deeds that are like mountains, and he will say, 'My Lord, how have I obtained this?' He will reply, 'By way of your child seeking forgiveness for you'.}'

1282) Al-Bayhaqī has narrated in *Shuʿab al-Īmān*, as well as ad-Daylamī, on the authority of Ibn ʿAbbās, who said, 'The Prophet ﷺ said: {There is no deceased in his grave except that he is like a drowning person looking for help. He waits for a supplication that will reach him from a father or a mother, or a child, or a trustworthy friend. If it reaches him, it is more beloved to him than the world and everything it contains. Indeed Allah enters the supplications of the people of the earth upon the people of the graves like mountains, and the gift of the living to the dead is seeking forgiveness for them.}' Al-Bayhaqī said, 'Abū ʿAlī al-Ḥusayn ibn ʿAlī al-Ḥāfiẓ said, "It is an uncommon (*gharīb*) ḥadīth from the ḥadīth of ʿAbdullah ibn Mubārak. It has not been found amongst the people of Khorasan".'

1283) Ibn Abī ad-Dunyā has narrated from Sufyān, who said, 'It has been said that the dead need supplications more than the living need food and drink'. Consensus that supplication benefits the deceased has been transmitted from more than one person, and the proof is Allah the Exalted's statement in the Qurʾān:

﴿وَٱلَّذِينَ جَآءُو مِنۢ بَعۡدِهِمۡ يَقُولُونَ رَبَّنَا ٱغۡفِرۡ لَنَا
وَلِإِخۡوَٰنِنَا ٱلَّذِينَ سَبَقُونَا بِٱلۡإِيمَٰنِ﴾

"Those who have come after them say, 'Our Lord, forgive us and our brothers who preceded us in faith'." [al-Ḥashr 59:10]

1284) Ibn Abī ad-Dunyā has narrated from someone of the First Three Generations, who said, 'I saw a brother of mine in my sleep after his death, so I said, "Do the supplications of the living reach you?" He replied, "Yes, by Allah. They shimmer like light and then we wear them".'

1285) He has also narrated from ʿAmr ibn Jarīr, who said, 'When the slave supplicates for his deceased brother, an angel brings it to him in his grave and says, "O inhabitant of the remote grave, this is a gift from a compassionate brother of yours".'

1286) Ibn Abī ad-Dunyā has narrated from Abū Qalābah, who said, 'I was heading towards Basra from the Levant. I dismounted at Khandaq, purified myself, and prayed two units[81] at night. Then I placed my head on a grave. Then I slept and then I woke up and there was the inhabitant of the grave complaining, saying, "You have harmed me since tonight". Then he said, "You do not know. We do know but we are not able to act. The two units that you prayed are better than the world and everything it contains". Then he said, "May Allah reward the people of the world with goodness. Convey our greetings of peace to them, for their supplications enter upon us as light like mountains".'

1287) Ibn Abī ad-Dunyā has narrated from one of the people of old, who said, 'I passed by the graves so I asked Allah to have mercy on them. Then a caller called out, "Yes, ask Allah to have mercy on them, for amongst them are the distressed and the grieved".'

1288) Ibn Rajab said, 'Jaʿfar al-Khuldī has related, "Al-ʿAbbās ibn Yaʿqūb ibn Ṣāliḥ al-Anbārī has narrated to us, 'I heard my father saying, "One of the righteous saw his father in his sleep, and he said to him, 'My dear son, why did you cut off your gift from us?' He replied, 'My dear father, do the deceased know the gift of the living?' He said, 'My dear son, were it not for the living, the deceased would be destroyed'."'"'

1289) Ibn an-Najjār has narrated in his *Tārīkh* from Mālik ibn Dīnār, who said, 'I entered the graveyard on Friday night and all of a sudden there was a light radiating therein, so I said, "There is no god but Allah. I wonder if Allah ﷻ has forgiven the people of the graves". Then, all of a sudden, a caller called out from the distance, saying, "O Mālik ibn Dīnār, this is the gift of the believers to their brothers from amongst the people of the graves". I said, "By the One Who made you speak, will you not tell me what it is?"' He replied, "A man from the believers got up tonight, did his ablution thoroughly, and prayed some units. In those units, he recited the opening chapter of the Book along with **"O you who disbelieve..."** and **"Say: 'He is**

81 Ar. *rakʿatayn*, sing. *rakʿah*.

Allah, Absolute Oneness..."[82] And he said,[83] 'O Allah, I have granted its reward to the believers from amongst the people of the graves', and thus Allah entered light and illumination upon us, and spaciousness and happiness, in the east and in the west."'

'Mālik said, 'I did not stop reciting them every Friday night. Then I saw the Prophet ﷺ in my sleep and he said to me, "O Mālik ibn Dīnār, Allah has forgiven you by the amount of light that you have granted to my Ummah, and you have the reward of that". Then he said to me, "Allah has built a house for you in Paradise, in a castle called *al-Manīf*". I said, "What is *al-Manīf*?" He replied, "It is that which overlooks the people of Paradise".'

1290) Ibn Abī ad-Dunyā has narrated from Bashshār ibn Ghālib, who said, 'I saw Rābiʿah in my sleep, and I would supplicate a lot for her. She said to me, "O Bashshār, your gifts come to us on plates covered in kerchiefs of silk". I said, "How is that?" She replied, "This is how the supplications of the living believers are when they supplicate for the deceased. He answers them and that supplication is put on plates of light, which are then covered with silk kerchiefs. Then it is brought to whomever from the deceased was supplicated for, and it is said to him, 'This is a gift for you from so-and-so'."'

1291) At-Ṭabarānī has narrated in *al-Awsaṭ* with a chain of transmission that he related from Anas *marfūʿan*: {My Ummah is an ummah that is shown mercy. They enter their graves with their sins and they come out of their graves without any sins. They are wiped out because of the believers' seeking forgiveness for them.}

1292) Ibn Abī Shaybah has narrated from al-Ḥasan, who said, 'It has reached me that in the Book of Allah: "Son of Adam; there are two things that I have made for you but they are not for you: making a bequest from your property in goodness, as

82 (tn): i.e. Sūrat al-Kāfirūn (109) and Sūrat al-Ikhlāṣ (112).
83 (tn): either in prostration or after the prayer (Dār al-Minhāj).

it will become someone else's property, and the Muslims supplicating for you while you are in an abode in which you cannot turn and repent from evil deeds or increase in good deeds".'

1293) Ad-Dārimī[84] has narrated in his *Musnad* on the authority of Ibn Masʿūd, who said, 'There are four things that the man is given after his death; a third of his wealth,[85] if it was done beforehand out of obedience to Allah, a righteous child who supplicates for him after his death, a good practice that the man established, and it is acted upon after his death, and one hundred people who intercede for him, and they are interceded for'.

1294) The two Sheikhs[86] have narrated on the authority of ʿĀʾishah ﷺ that a man said, 'O Messenger of Allah, my mother died suddenly and did not make a bequest. I think that if she had spoken, she would have given to charity. Would she thus get the reward if I gave to charity on her behalf?' He replied, {Yes.}[87]

1295) Al-Bukhārī[88] has narrated on the authority of Ibn ʿAbbās that Saʿd ibn ʿUbādah's mother died while he was absent, so he came to the Messenger of Allah ﷺ and said, 'O Messenger of Allah, my mother died while I was absent. Will it benefit her if I give to charity on her behalf?' He replied, {Yes.} He said, 'Then I make you a witness that my wall is charity on her behalf'.

1296) Aḥmad[89] and the Four[90] have narrated on the authority of Saʿd ibn ʿUbādah that he said, 'O Messenger of Allah, my mother has died. Which charity is the best?' He replied, {Water.} He thus dug a well and said, 'This is for Saʿd's mother'.

---

84 Narrated by ad-Dārimī in the Introduction in the chapter on whoever establishes a practice, good or bad (Ḥadīth 516).

85 (tn): i.e. as a bequest (*waṣiyyah*).

86 Narrated by al-Bukhārī in the Book of Funerals (Ḥadīth 1388) and narrated by Muslim in the Book of Zakāt in the chapter on the reward for charity reaching the deceased (Ḥadīth 1004).

87 (tn): A linguistic note has been omitted here.

88 Narrated by al-Bukhārī in the Book of Bequests (Ḥadīth 2756).

89 Narrated by Aḥmad in his *Musnad* (2/375).

90 Narrated by Abū Dāwūd in the Book of Zakāt in the chapter on the

1297) At-Ṭabarānī has narrated on the authority of ʿUqbah ibn ʿĀmir, who said, 'The Messenger of Allah ﷺ said, {Charity extinguishes the heat of the graves for its people.}'

1298) At-Ṭabarānī has narrated in *al-Awsaṭ* with an authentic chain of transmission on the authority of Anas ﷺ that Saʿd came to the Prophet ﷺ and said, 'O Messenger of Allah, my mother has died and she did not make a bequest. Would it benefit her if I gave charity on her behalf?' He replied: {Yes. Give water.}

1299) He has also narrated on the authority of Saʿd ibn ʿUbādah, who said, 'I said, "O Messenger of Allah, my mother has died and she did not make a bequest or give anything in charity. Would it benefit her if I gave charity on her behalf?" He replied: {Yes, even if it is a sheep's burnt trotter.}"'

1300) He has also narrated from Ibn ʿAmr, who said, 'The Messenger of Allah ﷺ said: {If one of you gives charity voluntarily and makes it on behalf of his parents, they will have its reward and his reward will not be decreased in the slightest.}'

1301) At-Ṭabarānī has narrated in *al-Awsaṭ* on the authority of Anas: 'I heard the Messenger of Allah ﷺ saying: {No member of a family dies and they give charity on his behalf after his death except that Jibrīl presents it to him on a plate of light. Then he stands on the edge of the grave and says, 'O inhabitant of the deep grave, this gift has been given to you by your family, so accept it'. Then it enters upon him and he rejoices and is delighted, while his neighbours who have not been gifted anything grieve.}

1302) Ibn Abī Shaybah has narrated from Saʿīd ibn Abī Saʿīd, who said, 'If a trotter is given in charity on behalf of a deceased, it will follow him'.[91]

---

virtue of giving water to drink (Ḥadīth 1431), narrated by an-Nasāʾī in the Book of Bequests (Ḥadīth 3604), and narrated by Ibn Mājah in the Book of Etiquette (Ḥadīth 3684). (tn): At-Tirmidhī (Ḥadīth 669) (Dār al-Minhāj).

91 (tn): i.e. he will get the reward.

1303) Al-Bayhaqī has narrated in *Shuʿab al-Īmān*, as well as al-Aṣbahānī in *at-Targhīb*, with a chain of transmission that contains two unknown persons (*majhūlān*),[92] on the authority of Ibn ʿUmar ﷺ who said, 'The Messenger of Allah ﷺ said: {Whoever performs a pilgrimage on behalf of his parents after their death, Allah prescribes that he is free from the Fire while those on whose behalf a pilgrimage is performed receive a complete pilgrimage (*ḥajjah tāmmah*) without having their reward diminished in the slightest.}'

And he ﷺ said: {A family member does not give anything to his fellow family member that is better than a pilgrimage that is done on his behalf after his death and he is in his grave.}

Abū ʿAbdillāh at-Thaqafī has narrated in his *Fawāʾid*, known as *ath-Thaqafiyyāt*, on the authority of Zayd ibn Arqam, from the Prophet ﷺ who said: {Whoever does a pilgrimage on behalf of his parents and they never did a pilgrimage, he is rewarded on their behalf, their spirits are given the glad tidings in the sky, and Allah records it as *birr*.}[93]

1304) Al-Bazzār has narrated, as well as at-Ṭabarānī, with a good chain of transmission on the authority of Anas, who said, 'A man came to the Prophet ﷺ and said, "My father has died and he did not perform the obligatory pilgrimage.[94]" He replied: {Have you not seen that if your father owes a debt, you pay it off on his behalf?} He said, 'Yes'. He replied: {It is a debt that he owes, so pay it off.}

1305) At-Ṭabarānī has narrated on the authority of ʿUqbah ibn ʿĀmir that a woman came to the Messenger of Allah ﷺ and said, 'Can I do the pilgrimage on behalf of my mother? She has died'. He replied: {Have you not seen that if your mother owes a debt, you pay it off? Is that not accepted from you?} She replied, 'Indeed'. He then commanded her to perform the pilgrimage.

92 (tn): which is a defect that renders the ḥadīth weak (*ḍaʿīf*), but it can be acted upon as it comes under virtuous actions (Dār al-Minhāj).

93 (tn): i.e. filial piety.

94 Ar. *ḥajjat al-Islām*, i.e. the Ḥajj that must be performed once in a believer's lifetime.

1306) And he has narrated in *al-Awsaṭ* on the authority of Abū Hurayrah ﷺ who said, 'The Messenger of Allah ﷺ said: {Whoever does a pilgrimage on behalf of a deceased, the one on whose behalf the pilgrimage is done gets the same reward.}'

1307) Ibn Abī Shaybah has narrated on the authority of ʿAṭāʾ and Yazīd ibn Aslam, who both said, 'A man came to the Prophet ﷺ and said, 'O Messenger of Allah, can I emancipate a slave on behalf of my father? He has died'. He replied, {Yes.}

1308) He has also narrated from ʿAṭāʾ, who said, 'After the deceased has died, emancipation, pilgrimage, and charity follow him'.

1309) He has also narrated from Abū Jaʿfar that al-Ḥasan and al-Ḥusayn would emancipate slaves on behalf of ʿAlī after his death.

1310) Ibn Saʿd has narrated from al-Qāsim ibn Muḥammad that ʿĀʾishah emancipated a slave on behalf of her brother ʿAbdur Raḥmān, from his old property, hoping that it would benefit him after his death.

1311) Abū ash-Sheikh Ibn Ḥayyān has narrated in the book *al-Waṣāyā* on the authority of ʿAmr ibn al-ʿĀṣ that he said, 'O Messenger of Allah, al-ʿĀṣ advised that one hundred people be emancipated on his behalf, and Hishām has emancipated fifty of them'. He ﷺ replied: {No. Giving charity, the pilgrimage, and emancipation are only done on behalf of the Muslim. If he had been Muslim, it would have reached him.}

1312) Ibn Abī Shaybah has narrated on the authority of al-Ḥajjāj ibn Dīnār, who said, 'The Messenger of Allah ﷺ said: {Indeed the *birr* after the *birr* is to prayer over the two of them with your prayer, fast on their behalf along with their fasting and give charity on their behalf along with your charity.}'

1313) Muslim[95] has narrated on the authority of Buraydah that a woman said, 'O Messenger of Allah, my mother was supposed to fast two months. Can I fast them on her behalf?' He replied: {Yes.} She then said, 'My mother did the pilgrimage. Can I do it on her behalf?' He said: {Yes.}

1314) The two Sheikhs[96] have narrated on the authority of ʿĀʾishah, who said, 'The Messenger of Allah ﷺ said, {Whoever dies and owes a fast, let his guardian fast on his behalf.}'

1315) There has been a difference of opinion as to whether the reward of recitation reaches the deceased. The majority of the First Three Generations and the three Imams hold that it reaches, while our Imam, ash-Shāfiʿī, differed, and his proof was the Exalted's statement,

﴿وَأَن لَّيْسَ لِلْإِنسَـٰنِ إِلَّا مَا سَعَىٰ﴾

"that man will have nothing but what he strives for. [an-Najm 53:39]

The former have responded to the āyah with the following approaches:

1. **The first** is that the āyah is abrogated by the Exalted's statement,

   ﴿وَٱتَّبَعَتْهُمْ ذُرِّيَّتُهُم بِإِيمَـٰنٍ﴾

   "And we will unite those who believed with their offspring" [at-Ṭūr 52:21] and the rest of the āyah. Children are put into Paradise because of the righteousness of parents.

95 Narrated by Muslim in the Book of Fasting in the chapter on making up fasts for the deceased (Ḥadīth 1149).

96 Narrated by al-Bukhārī in the Book of Fasting in the chapter on whoever dies owing a fast (Ḥadīth 1952) and narrated by Muslim in the Book of Fasting in the chapter on making up fasts for the deceased (Ḥadīth 1147).

2. **The second** is that it applies exclusively to the people of Ibrāhīm and the people of Mūsā, upon them be peace. As for this Ummah, they have what they strive for and what others strive for on their behalf. This was stated by ʿIkrimah.

3. **The third** is that what is meant by man here is the disbeliever. As for the believer, he has what he strives for and what others strive for on his behalf. This was stated by ar-Rabīʿ Ibn Anas.

4. **The fourth** is that man only has what he strives for by way of justice. As for anything extra, then it is possible for Allah the Exalted to increase it however much He wills. This was stated by al-Ḥusayn ibn al-Faḍl.

5. **The fifth** is that the *lām* in *lil insān* (**"...man will have..."**) actually means *ʿalā* (upon), and therefore man will have nothing upon him except what he strives for.

They also infer that it reaches by making an analogy of what has been mentioned by way of supplication, charity, fasting, the pilgrimage, and supplication, for there is no difference in transferring the reward whether it be a pilgrimage, charity, an endowment (*waqf*), supplication or recitation.

They also infer from the aḥādīth that mention it, even though they are weak, for their sum total indicates that there is a foundation. Furthermore, the Muslims in every big city still gather together and recite for the benefit of their deceased without any reproach. Thus, it is a consensus. All of this has been mentioned by al-Ḥāfiẓ Shams ad-Dīn ibn ʿAbdul Wāḥid al-Maqdasī al-Ḥanbalī in a volume he wrote on the issue.

Al-Qurṭubī said, 'Ash-Sheikh ʿIzz ad-Dīn ibn ʿAbdis Salām would issue *fatāwā* stating the reward for what one recites does not reach the deceased. When he had died, one of his companions saw him, so he said to him, "You used to say the reward for what one recites does not reach the deceased and is not gifted to him, so how is it?" He replied, "I used to say that in the abode of the world. Now, I have gone back on my position after seeing Allah's magnanimity therein and that it does reach him".'

As for reciting over the grave, our companions and others have decisively affirmed its legitimacy. Az-Zaʿfarānī said, 'I asked ash-Shāfiʿī about reciting over the grave and he said, "There is no harm in it".'

An-Nawawī has stated in *Sharḥ al-Muhadhdhib*, 'It is recommended for the visitor of the graves to recite what he can from the Qurʾān and to supplicate for them afterwards. This is the strongest position of ash-Shāfiʿī and what the companions have agreed upon'.

And he added in another place, 'And if they complete the Qurʾān over the grave, that's better'.[97]

Imam Aḥmad ibn Ḥanbal initially rejected it, as no tradition (*athar*) had reached him on the matter, but when it did he went back on his position. Some of what has been mentioned can be found above in the chapter on what is said at the time of burial, such as the ḥadīth of Ibn ʿUmar and al-ʿAlāʾ ibn al-Lajlāj, both of them *marfūʿan*.

1317) Al-Khallāl has narrated in *al-Jāmiʿ* on the authority of ash-Shaʿbī, who said, 'When one of the Helpers died, they would frequent his grave and recite the Qurʾān for him'.

1318) Abū Muḥammad as-Samarqandī has narrated in *Faḍāʾil Qul Huw Allahu Aḥad*[98] on the authority of ʿAlī *marfūʿan*: {Whoever passes by the graves and recites *Qul Huw Allahu Aḥad* eleven times and then donates its reward to the deceased is given a reward according to the number of deceased.}

97 (tn): *al-Majmūʿ Sharḥ al-Muhadhdhib* (5/254) (Dār al-Minhāj).

98 (tn): i.e. Sūrat al-Ikhlāṣ (112).

1319) Abū al-Qāsim ibn ʿAlī az-Zanjānī has narrated in his *Fawāʾid* on the authority of Abū Hurayrah, who said, 'The Messenger of Allah ﷺ said: {Whoever enters the graveyards and then recites the opening chapter of the Book along with *Qul Huw Allahu Aḥad* and *Alhākum at-Takāthur*[99] and then says, 'I have donated the reward for what I have recited from Your Speech to the believing men and women from amongst the people of the graves', they will intercede for him before Allah the Exalted.}

1320) Al-Qāḍī Abū Bakr ibn ʿAbdul Bāqī al-Anṣārī has narrated in his *Mashyakhah* from Salamah ibn ʿUbayd, who said, 'Ḥammād al-Makkī said, "I went out to the graves of Makkah one night and I placed my head on a grave and then slept. Then I saw the people of the graves standing in circles, so I said, 'Has the Standing been established?' They replied, 'No, but a man from our brothers recited *Qul Huwa Allahu Aḥad* and donated the reward to us, and we have been distributing it amongst ourselves for a year'."'

1321) ʿAbdul ʿAzīz, the companion of al-Khallāl, has narrated with his own chain of transmission on the authority of Anas ﷺ that the Messenger of Allah ﷺ said: {Whoever enters the graveyards and recites Sūrat Yā Sīn, Allah grants them relief and good deeds are written for him according to the number of people therein.}

1322) Al-Qurṭubī has said regarding the ḥadīth: {Recite Yā Sīn over your deceased}, 'This recitation could be done when the person is dying and it could be when he is in his grave'.

I say: The former is what the majority have stated, as has already been mentioned at the beginning of this book,[100] while the latter has been stated by Ibn ʿAbdul Wāḥid al-Maqdasī in the aforementioned volume. The position that it applies to both situations has been stated by al-Muḥibb at-Ṭabarī from amongst our latter companions.

---

99 (tn): i.e. Sūrat at-Takāthur (102).

100 (tn): Please see chapter 12.

And in the *Iḥyā'* of al-Ghazālī, as well as *al-ʿĀqibah* of ʿAbdul Ḥaqq ibn Aḥmad ibn Ḥanbal, he states, 'When you enter the graveyards, recite the opening chapter of the Book, *al-Muʿawwidhatān*[101] and *Qul Huwa Allahu Aḥad* and donate it to the people of the graves, for indeed it will reach them'.

1323) Al-Qurṭubī has said, 'It has been said that the reward of the recitation is for the reciter while the deceased gets the reward of listening, and this is why he receives mercy. The Exalted has said,

﴿وَإِذَا قُرِئَ ٱلْقُرْءَانُ فَٱسْتَمِعُوا لَهُۥ وَأَنصِتُوا لَعَلَّكُمْ تُرْحَمُونَ﴾

"When the Qur'ān is recited, listen to it and be quiet so that hopefully you will gain mercy." [al-'Aʿrāf 7:204]'

He also said, 'It is not improbable, in the magnanimity of Allah the Exalted, for Him to grant him the reward of both the recitation and the listening, and to grant him the reward of whatever recitation is gifted to him even if he did not hear it, just like charity and supplication'.

And in the *Fatāwā* of Qāḍī Khān from amongst the Ḥanafīs: 'Whoever recites the Qur'ān in the presence of graves and by doing so has the intention that the sound of the Qur'ān bring ease to them, then he recites, and if he does not intend that then Allah hears the recitation wherever it is'.

101 (tn): i.e. Sūrat al-Falaq (113) and Sūrat an-Nās (114).

Section

1324) Al-Qurṭubī has said, 'One of our scholars, in showing that the deceased benefit from recitation at the grave, has used the ḥadīth of the *ʿasīb*[102] which the Prophet ﷺ split into two, planted, and said: {Maybe it will be mitigated for them until they dry.}'

Al-Khaṭṭābī has said, 'According to the people of knowledge, this is understood to mean that as long as things are as they were originally created or still have their greenness and freshness then they glorify until their moistness dries, or their greenness changes or they are cut from their root'.[103]

1325) Someone other than al-Khaṭṭābī, has said, 'If it was mitigated for them because of the glorification of the *jarīd*,[104] then what about the believer reciting the Qurʾān?'[105] He also said, 'And this ḥadīth is the foundation for planting trees by graves'.

1326) Ibn ʿAsākir has narrated from the path of Ḥammād ibn Salamah from Qatādah that Abū Barzah al-Aslamī ؓ would narrate that the Messenger of Allah ﷺ passed by a grave and its inhabitant was being punished, so he took a *jarīdah*, planted it in the grave and said, {Perhaps it will mitigate it for him as long as it is moist.}Thus, Abū Barzah would advise, 'When I die, put me in my grave along with two palm branches stripped of their leaves'. He[106] said, 'He then died in a desert between Kerman and Qumis, and they said, "He advised us to put two palm branches stripped of their leaves in his grave, but they do not exist in this place". While they were in that situation, a

102 (tn): i.e. a palm branch stripped of its leaves.
103 (tn): This is based on the āyah: ﴿وَإِن مِّن شَيْءٍ إِلَّا يُسَبِّحُ بِحَمْدِهِ﴾ **"There is nothing which does not glorify him with praise"** [al-Isrāʾ 17:44] (Dār al-Minhāj).
104 (tn): i.e. palm branches stripped of their leaves.
105 (tn): 'Imam an-Nawawī ؒ stated this in *Sharḥ Muslim* (3/202) and he said, "The scholars have recommended reciting the Qurʾān at the grave because of this ḥadīth..."' (Dār al-Minhāj).
106 (tn): i.e. Qatādah.

travelling party appeared from the direction of Sistan (*Sijistān*) and they had some palm fronds with them, so they stripped two branches from them and put them in his grave with him'.

1327) Ibn Saᶜd has narrated from Muwarriq, who said, 'Buraydah advised that two palm branches stripped of their leaves be put in his grave'.

And in *Tārīkh Ibn an-Najjār* in the biography of Kathīr ibn Sālim al-Hītī, it is mentioned that he advised that his grave not be rebuilt if it is obliterated, and he heavily stressed it and emphasised it. He said, 'Indeed Allah, Mighty and Majestic is He, looks at the inhabitants of obliterated graves and has mercy on them, so I hope to be among them'.[107]

Ibn an-Najjār said, 'The like of what he said has been in the traditions'.

Then he narrated from the path of ᶜAbd ibn Ḥamīd, who said, 'Ismāᶜīl ibn ᶜAbdul Karīm narrated to us, "ᶜAbd as-Ṣamad ibn Maᶜqal narrated to us from Wahb ibn Munabbih, who said, 'The Prophet Jeremiah ﷺ passed by some graves whose inhabitants were being punished. A year later, he passed by the same graves and the punishment had subsided. He said, "Quddūs, Quddūs, I passed by these graves a year ago and its inhabitants were being punished. I passed by this year and the punishment had subsided!" Then there was a call from the sky, "O Jeremiah, their shrouds have been ripped, their hair has been pulled out and their graves have been obliterated. I thus looked at them and had mercy on them. This is what I do with the people whose graves have been obliterated, whose shrouds have been ripped and whose hair has been pulled out".'"'

107 (tn): 'And there is no harm in marking a grave, because the Prophet ﷺ marked the grave of ᶜUthmān ibn Maẓᶜūn with a rock and said, {So that I can gather his brothers with him.}' (Dār al-Minhāj).

Appendix B

Benefitting the Deceased

by Imam Yaḥyā an-Nawawī[108]

30: The Chapter on How the Statements of Others Benefit the Deceased

The ʿulamāʾ have made consensus that supplicating (*duʿāʾ*) for the deceased benefits them and the reward for it reaches them. Their proof is Allah the Exalted's words:

﴿وَٱلَّذِينَ جَآءُو مِنۢ بَعْدِهِمْ يَقُولُونَ رَبَّنَا ٱغْفِرْ لَنَا
وَلِإِخْوَٰنِنَا ٱلَّذِينَ سَبَقُونَا بِٱلْإِيمَـٰنِ﴾

"And those who came into the faith after them say, 'Our Lord, forgive us and our brothers who went before us in faith'." [al-Ḥashr 59:10] and other well-known āyāt that bear the same meaning, and well-known aḥādīth:

486) such as his ﷺ words: {O Allah, forgive the people of *Baqīʿ al-Gharqad*} [Muslim, 974]

487) as well as his ﷺ words: {O Allah, forgive our living and our dead.}[109]

---

108 Translated from *Al-Adhkār Min Kalām Sayyid Al-Abrār* by al-Imām, al-ʿAlāmah, al-Mujtahid, Muḥyī ad-Dīn Abū Zakariyyā Yaḥyā Ibn Sharaf An-Nawawī (Jeddah: Dār al-Minhāj, 2012/1433), 283-284. This translation was originally published on Mahdi Lock's blog.

109 (tn): This is part of a longer ḥadīth that Imam an-Nawawī quotes earlier in *al-Adhkār*, no. 472. It is found in *Sunan Abī Dāwūd* (no. 3201), *Sunan at-Tirmidhī* (no. 1024), *Sunan al-Bayhaqī* (4/41), and the *Mustadrak* of al-Ḥākim (1/358). Imam al-Ḥākim said, 'This ḥadīth is *ṣaḥīḥ* according to the conditions of Al-Bukhārī and Muslim'. See p.271-272 of *al-Adhkār* for further details.

The ʿulamāʾ have differed over whether the reward for reciting the Qurʾān reaches the deceased. The dominant (*mashhūr*) position of the Shāfiʿī madhhab, as well as a group of other scholars, is that it does not reach, while Aḥmad ibn Ḥanbal and a group of scholars, as well as a group of scholars from the Shāfiʿī madhhab, hold the position that it does reach. The one reciting may say once he has finished, 'O Allah, give the reward of what I have read to so-and-so',[110] and Allah knows best.[111] It is recommended to praise the deceased and mention their merits and good qualities.

488) In the two *Ṣaḥīḥ* collections of al-Bukhārī and Muslim, we have related on the authority of Anas ﷺ, who said, 'They passed by a *janāzah* and the people were saying good things about the person, and then The Prophet ﷺ said: {It is necessary (*wajabat*).} Then they passed by another *janāzah* and the people were saying evil things about the person. Again, he said: {It is necessary.} Then, ʿUmar bin Al-Khaṭṭāb ﷺ said, "What is necessary?" He said: {You said good things about this person, so Paradise is necessary for him, and you said evil things about this other person, so the Fire is necessary for him. You are Allah's witnesses on earth.}'

489) In the *Ṣaḥīḥ* of al-Bukhārī, we have related on the authority of Abū Al-Aswad, who said, 'I arrived in al-Madīnah and sat with ʿUmar bin Al-Khaṭṭāb ﷺ when a *janāzah* passed by. The people were saying good things about the person, so ʿUmar said, "It is necessary". Then another *janāzah* passed by and again, good things were said about the person, so ʿUmar said, "It is necessary". Then a third *janāzah* passed by and bad things were said about the person, so ʿUmar said, "It is necessary".' Abū al-Aswad said, 'I said, "What is necessary, O Commander of the Believers?" He said: "I have said as the Prophet ﷺ said: {If four people testify to the goodness of any Muslim, Allah will enter him into Paradise.} We said: 'And three?' He said: {And

110 Ar. *Allahumm awṣil thawāba ma qaraʾtuhu ilā* [enter name here].

111 (tn): For further details on this point, please read Imam Wahbah az-Zuḥaylī's fatwā in Appendix C.

three.} We said: 'And two?' He said: {And two.} Then we did not ask about one.'" The aḥādīth that are similar to what we have mentioned are many, and Allah knows best.

Appendix C

Fatwā on Reciting the Qur'ān for the Deceased

by Imam Wahbah az-Zuḥaylī[112]

Question: Does the reward of the Fātiḥah and reciting other parts of the Qur'ān reach the deceased after they have died or after they have been buried in their graves or any other place?

Answer: There are two conflicting opinions on this matter that have been mentioned by as-Sanʿānī in his book *Bushra al-Ka'īb bi Liqā' al-Ḥabīb.*

The **first opinion**, which is the dominant (*mashhūr*) opinion of the madhhabs of Mālik and ash-Shāfiʿī, is that it does not reach.

The **second opinion**, which is the madhhab of Imam Aḥmad and the majority of the First Three Generations (*as-Salaf*) and the four madhabs, including the later Mālikīs and Shāfiʿīs, is that the reward does reach. Imām Abū Ḥanīfah said. 'The deceased receives everything from *ṣadaqa* and whatever else'. He also said, 'Read "Āyat al-Kursī" three times and *Qul Huwa Allahu Aḥad*[113] and say, "O Allah, indeed the bounty (*faḍl*) is for the people of the graves".'

112 Translated from *Fatāwā Muʿāṣirah* by Imam Wahbah az-Zuḥaylī, (Damascus: Dar Al-Fikr, 2003), 273-274. The translation of this fatwa was originally published on Mahdi Lock's blog.
113 (tn): i.e. the 112th sūrah.

As-Sanʿānī mentioned the proofs for the second opinion, whose proponents say that the deceased benefit from what the living do for them, from the Book, the Sunnah, consensus (*ijmāʾ*), and the principles of the Revealed Law.

As for the Book, it is the Exalted One's words: **"And those who came into the faith after them say, 'Our Lord, forgive us and our brothers who went before us in faith'."** [al-Ḥashr 59:10] Allah praised them because they sought forgiveness for the believers who came before them, and this proves that the deceased benefit from the living's seeking forgiveness. The deceased's benefitting from supplication [*duʾā*] is also proved by the consensus of the Ummah regarding supplicating for them in the *janāzah* prayer.

The aḥādīth have confirmed that he ﷺ supplicated in the *janāzah* prayer for whoever sent prayers upon him, and he said: {O Allah, forgive him, have mercy on him, excuse him and pardon him.}[114]

Consensus has been made stating that it is permissible for a debt to be discharged on behalf of a deceased person by anyone, close or far, and that if the deceased owes a debt to a living person, that person can waive it and no longer make any claim to it, just as he would with a living person. Consensus has also been made stating that since the reward for fasting (whether voluntary or obligatory) reaches the deceased and it is confirmed in the Sunnah, it is thus proven that the reward for all other actions reaches them. The texts have confirmed that the reward reaches the deceased for three kinds of worship: physical (i.e. fasting), financial (giving charity on behalf of the dead), and the physical and the financial combined (through performing the Hajj on behalf of a deceased person or someone who is chronically ill and unable to move).

114 Narrated by al-Bukhārī in *Al-Adab* as well as Muslim, Abū Dāwūd, At-Tirmidhī, and an-Nasāʾī from Abū Hurayrah.

Ibn Taymiyyah[115] said, 'Indeed the deceased benefit from the recitation of Qurʾān as they benefit from financial worship such as charity (*ṣadaqa*) and other things'. Likewise, an-Nawawī said in *Al-Majmūʿ*,[116] 'The reward for reciting the Qurʾān reaches the deceased'.

In conclusion, the relied-upon (*muʿtamad*) position of the Four Madhhabs is that the reward for reciting the Qurʾān reaches the deceased if the living dedicate it to them.

115 (tn): i.e. Taqī ud-Dīn Ahmad ibn Taymiyyah.
116 (tn): This is Imām an-Nawawī's 27-volume fiqh book, which is the ultimate reference work for the Shāfiʿī school.

Printed in Great Britain
by Amazon

30637551R00047